WOMEN
AT WAR 1939–1945
THE HOME FRONT

CAROL HARRIS

SUTTON PUBLISHING

First published in 2000 by
Sutton Publishing Limited · Phoenix Mill
Thrupp · Stroud · Gloucestershire · GL5 2BU

Reprinted in 2001, 2003

British Library Cataloguing in Publication Data
A catalogue record for this book is available from the British Library

ISBN 0 7509 2536 1

Flexible working patterns and childcare schemes were widespread during the Second World War.

Typeset in 11/12 pt Ehrhardt.
Typesetting and origination by
Sutton Publishing Limited.
Printed and bound in England by
J.H. Haynes & Co. Ltd, Sparkford.

Contents

Acknowledgements

I am grateful to the many people who have supported and contributed to the project, especially the following:

Mary Archer, Sheila Ashton (née Wigham), Diana Barnato Walker, Bridget Bolwig, Nellie Brook, Mary Buck (née Blackburn), Carol Burton, Roger Campion, Bertha Catesby, Iris Cawthorne, 'Ninkey' Coe, Vera Costan, Joyce Crang, Mabel Dutton, Alice Mary Ewing, Jonathan Falconer, Edith Fox, Nancy Furlong, Eddie Gardner, Annice Gibbs, John Gilman, Kitty Goff, Peter Good, Marjorie Goodliffe, Paula Hamer, Robina Hinton, Gwen Holland, Elizabeth Jackson, John Kirk, Moira Macleod, Marjorie Meath, George V. Monk, Olive Owens (née Stevenson), Madge Parnell, Margaret Peer, Doreen Perkins, J. Pritchard, Doreen Rapley (née Crane), Gladys Reeves, Susan Sear, Margaret Stevenson (née Westley), Alma Teague, Pat Vaughan (née Berry), Iris Walters (née Daniels), Betty Wilson, Joan Young.

Special thanks to William and Ralph for their patience, and to Michael Brown for all his help.

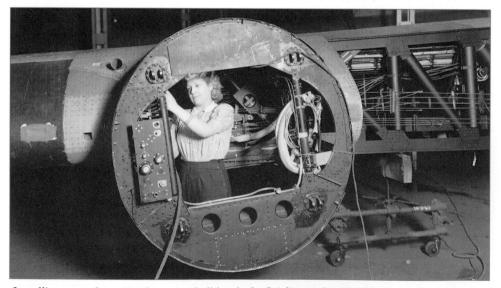

Installing control runs on the engine bulkhead of a Stirling at Longbridge shadow factory, March 1943. (Rover Group/Jonathan Falconer Collection)

Introduction

The civilian population of Britain was involved in the Second World War as it had never been before in an international conflict. This did not just mean coping with air raids and rationing. Even before the start of hostilities, official calculations indicated that the country would be seriously short of the manpower it needed to fight the enemy and to keep up production of weapons, food and the other essentials of everyday life. Female volunteers working in specified areas and with particular duties, it was hoped, would fill the gap.

Typically, the Government and the military looked back to the previous conflict for ideas. During the First World War, women had volunteered for factory and munitions work, as well as jobs on the buses, on the land and in the forces, and official thinking was that something similar would suffice again. So women were urged to put themselves forward. Once more they replaced workers on farms and in factories and carried out non-combatant roles such as driving and clerical duties in the forces. A new organisation, the Women's Voluntary Service, was created in 1938 to coordinate and support the work of other voluntary organisations in Civil Defence.

But if the initial blueprint was based on the First World War, it quickly became apparent that if Britain was to stand any chance of meeting the required levels of production and strength in its fighting forces, women would have to be compulsorily involved. Rules about limited duties and age limits that initially called on young, single women were revised and broadened. By 1941, the Government had to face the facts that most others had recognised long before: any effective response would have to involve the wholesale conscription of women.

In 1944, *Man Power*, the official Government publication on the mobilisation of Britain, commented: 'The whole business of mobilising and employing women – wives, sweethearts, daughters – is new and tricky. It creates special and dangerous problems of its own, over and above those encountered in the conscription and mobilisation of men.'

Whatever these difficulties, perceived or imaginary, of just over 33 million people aged between fourteen and sixty-four living in Britain in 1944, over half were women. By this time, the conscription scheme had grown to the point where just about every girl and woman in Britain between the ages of fourteen and sixty-four had a job to do in addition to looking after their children and families, which many were doing single-handedly. Most women were married. There were

9,000,000 children, almost entirely in the care of women. Behind these bald facts and figures were millions of women working long hours in paid employment or as volunteers – many of them taking on both roles. Flexible working patterns and nurseries for mothers of young children became widespread, so that even they could make their contribution to the war effort.

A common theme on the Home Front was the sometimes uneasy relationship between the women of Britain and the Government. Often, the women themselves identified needs and the practical solutions to meet them which the Government was loathe to acknowledge. Despite official disapproval, for example, many learned rifle-shooting and unarmed combat, or how to make Molotov cocktails (petrol bombs) and throw grenades to ward off the invader. And although everyone had to do something, the various ministries realised early on that there was little point in trying to force women to be where they did not want to go. Even though they were conscripted, women civilians exercised fully their right to say what they would and would not do. In this respect at least, many found life very different when they later volunteered for the forces.

Women also voluntarily collected ton after ton of salvage, knitted, sewed and raised money for warships, Spitfires and tanks, the Red Cross and other good causes. They looked after their own and other people's children either locally or as evacuees and accommodated people whose homes had been bombed. Many who held down day jobs volunteered as air-raid wardens and fire-watchers in their time off duty. They ran fire stations, worked as rat-catchers and drove ambulances, ferrying casualties to hospital while cities burned and enemy bombs exploded around them. They kept their families going, often as single parents, while their husbands were away for protracted periods, fighting in the armed forces.

However, the women of wartime Britain, despite campaigns that have attracted widespread public support, still have no memorial statue or other acknowledgement that without their enormous and crucial contribution, the lives we live now would be very different. These were extraordinary times in which ordinary women did extraordinary things and I have tried to cover as many aspects of life for civilian women as possible. Inevitably, space has meant that I have not been able to include a great deal of the fascinating material I have received. But to everyone who shared their memories and lent precious photographs, thank you for your contributions – then and now.

CHAPTER 1
Conscription and Direction

As the First World War ended, British women who had responded to the call made in 1916 to volunteer for work in factories, on buses, in shops, offices and the like were told it was now their duty to return to the home. To emphasise this point, women were prohibited from claiming unemployment benefit and trade-union pressures ensured their dismissal from a wide range of industries, including engineering, printing, transport and munitions. Even in fields where a woman could traditionally expect to find work, such as the civil service or in nursing, it was expected that she would relinquish her job on marriage.

The contribution of British women during the First World War did, however, have some lasting effects. First and foremost, away from their husbands, fathers, brothers and boyfriends, many had experienced a previously unimaginable level of independence, as well as increased responsibilities. Fashions reflected changes as trousers and shorter skirts, initially worn by women because they were practical necessities in many jobs, became fashionable in their own right. The well-to-do Edwardian woman's habit of changing her clothes several times a day had quickly become unpatriotic, as had ostentation in dress. Women experimented more with their cosmetics, and a fashion for heavy make-up became popular, in the style of film stars Pola Negri and Theda Bara. This scandalised the older generation, especially when lipstick, rouge and powder were applied in public. Further outrage was caused in the 1930s when, encouraged by tobacco companies, women started smoking in public.

On the political front, women's contributions to the war effort between 1916 and 1918 bolstered immeasurably their campaign for the right to vote. Finally, in 1928, the franchise was fully extended to women, giving them the vote on the same terms as men. Wartime working experience had expanded opportunities for women who would otherwise have inevitably entered domestic service. The change was permanent: servant shortages in this post-war era were resolved partly through the introduction of labour-saving gadgets and partly through the evolution of smaller, suburban middle-class homes. Women were admitted for the first time to a number of professions, including the Bar, and benefited from reforms to taxation and matrimonial laws.

Inevitably, such rapid and major upheavals were not universally welcomed. In the 1920s, people despaired of the morals and preoccupations of young people and in particular, the young women known as 'Flappers' and 'Jazz Babies'. A 'Flapper' in the late nineteenth century was a very young prostitute but by the outbreak of the First World War, it applied to any young girl with a boyish figure. After the war, this youthful shape was even more popular as the desired form for fashionable young women and the term was generally used to describe any 'comradely, sporting and active young woman', according to social commentators Robert Graves and Alan Hodge, writing in 1939. 'Jazz Babies' were a 1920s variation on the 'Flappers' – they were young women who danced to the new and frenetic jazz music of American musicians such as Louis Armstrong and Fats Waller, who were enormously popular and frequently toured Britian and Europe. The popular image of this 'Lost Generation', particularly its sexual mores, drunkenness and drug-taking, was representative of only a small minority, even of those with the means and the inclination. But the tabloid press did its level best to expose in full, lurid, shocked and shocking detail the exploits of the happy few.

More prosaically, until the 1920s, most women expected child-rearing and domestic duties to dominate their lives after marriage. But in this decade, married women could for the first time obtain contraception at clinics set up by Marie Stopes, whose best-selling book, *Married Love*, changed the lives of, especially, working class women and those living in poverty. Underpinning Dr Stopes' approach was her commitment to eugenics. Her aim, in common with many other thinkers across the political and social spectrum in Europe at that time, was racial purity. This meant those who did not meet what was deemed an acceptable standard either physically, mentally or morally had to be bred out of the race. Regardless of Dr Stopes' motives, these developments meant, for the first time, that ordinary women could see an alternative to serial pregnancy, and therefore an alternative to the financially and physically debilitating effects that larger families inevitably entailed.

So the horizons of women born just before, during and after the First World War were far wider than those of their mothers. Work outside the home in a range of occupations was a practical possibility, in different ways, for women of all classes. As the slump and depression of the 1920s and 1930s seriously affected male employment, women spurred on by both necessity and opportunity took up paid work when their husbands could find none. Many of the better off continued to be active in the voluntary sphere, which had blossomed through flag days and other fund-raising events during the First World War. The depression of the 1920s and 1930s gave them plenty of opportunities to contribute.

" So, actually, all you're doing at the moment is the housework, arranging and cooking meals for your husband, children and evacuees, canteen work and voluntary fire watching ? "

The frequent tension between usually younger, single, female interviewers and interviewees is well documented, here by Daily Herald *cartoonist Gilbert Wilkinson.*

The first major task of Women's Voluntary Services was planning the evacuation of children from areas at risk of aerial bombardment, which was expected from the day war broke out. The services they had in mind included organising communal feeding, departure and reception of children, billeting and keeping check on those involved. (HMSO)

As the 1930s progressed, then, women of all classes were working in increasing numbers. When the Second World War broke out, in September 1939, nearly 5 million were in paid employment in the United Kingdom. Preparations for war had begun in earnest long before the Munich Crisis of 1938: tens of thousands of women volunteers already had jobs to do, for example, in the Auxiliary Fire Service, as wardens in Air Raid Precautions or with the Women's Voluntary Service (later the Women's Royal Voluntary Service). More women than men had volunteered at this early stage. The WVS organised the first evacuation of children away from cities at high risk from bombing in October 1938, after the Munich Crisis and again one year later, just after war broke out in 1939.

Internment was introduced for home-grown Nazi sympathisers and all 'enemy aliens', many of whom had fled to Britain to escape Nazi persecution. The national mood alternated between hysteria at the potential havoc that could be wreaked by fifth columnists and unease at imprisoning people who were clearly anti-fascist, simply because they were foreigners. Despite the national unease, however, many internees were remarkably generous in their attitude towards this new and, for some, terrifying turn of events. At the age of twenty-five, Paula Hamer came from her home, a farm in Germany, to work in England as a children's nurse. When war broke out, she was interned.

I had been here for nine months when the war started. I was interned in Holloway. There were 182 of us – including a Swiss girl, next door to me, who could not speak a word of English.

You got porridge for breakfast with marge, bread and tea and they always had urns of boiling water available so you could make yourself hot chocolate or tea whenever you wanted. We were treated differently to the other prisoners and were put on one or two floors especially allocated for internees.

We could do what we wanted – really, you would be surprised. I worked in the hospital and the library and did the sewing. On Saturdays and Sundays, we served prison officers and the ladies their lunch. We were paid sixpence a day for that.

Her petition to be released was allowed and for the rest of the war Paula Hamer was a member of the fire service, based in Kensington.

For all its willingness to encourage women to come forward for voluntary work, when war broke out in September 1939 the Government was reluctant to bring them into the workforce, in part because, with considerable justification, it feared union opposition. On the other hand, it recognised that calling up working men for active service, and expanding those industries specifically linked to armaments, would create a labour shortage. The Government hoped initially to draw on the pool of unemployed men and those men whose work would be curtailed by the outbreak of war. Women would also be needed, it believed, in much the same way as they filled the breach in the conflict twenty years earlier. This meant limited activities in the auxiliary forces and on the Home Front, mainly to release men for active service.

Early in 1939, just before the outbreak of war, the Government published *National Service*, subtitled 'A guide to the ways in which the people of this country may give service.' It lists ARP, especially the Women's Voluntary Service, Auxiliary Fire Service, the Red Cross, Auxiliary Territorial Service, Royal Air Force companies and the Civil Air Guard, as being particularly suitable for women, and offered part-time training for volunteers. Work deemed particularly suitable for women and not needing advanced training included the Women's Land Army, service in the Royal Navy and Auxiliary Hospital Service and help in evacuating children from dangerous areas. In addition, the Government set up a Central Bureau for men and women with professional and technical qualifications to work where needed, as directed by the Government.

A rather glamorous image, typical of the way women, both volunteers and conscripts, were portrayed during the Second World War.

Women volunteered in substantial numbers but more significant were those who argued that they had too many new responsibilities in the home and at work to offer any meaningful free time. By 1940, it was becoming clear that women would not bridge the gap voluntarily. One of the first steps was to convert volunteers, male and female, in Civil Defence and other areas into a compulsory workforce by 'freezing' their posts. This meant that the erstwhile volunteers, justly proud of their decision to opt in, could no longer opt out by resigning. It sparked some resentment among those who had volunteered in the early days of the war, and so they were given a fortnight's grace during which they could resign.

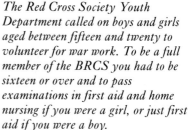

The Red Cross Society Youth Department called on boys and girls aged between fifteen and twenty to volunteer for war work. To be a full member of the BRCS you had to be sixteen or over and to pass examinations in first aid and home nursing if you were a girl, or just first aid if you were a boy.

While there was much grumbling about the change, everyone realised that resignation would only make one eligible for compulsory deployment in another capacity, so few took the opportunity to leave. In May, agreement was reached with the main trade unions to admit women to various kinds of work. A turning point was the secret report prepared by Sir William Beveridge and presented in late 1940. It spelled out the looming labour crisis in hard figures. Men would be required in increasing numbers in Civil Defence and the armed forces. To meet this need, they would have to be withdrawn from industries, most crucially munitions, which would itself have to expand to meet the growing wartime demand. The shortfall was frankly enormous: 1½ million women would have to be added to the workforce to maintain production at the necessary levels.

In spring 1941, the first woman registered under the Registration for Employment Order. By August 1941, 87,000 women out of a potential workforce of 2 million had found work in auxiliary services and munitions. This compared poorly with the 175,000 women who had become unemployed in 1939 as a result of cutbacks in non-essential industries. Ernest Bevin, the Minister of Labour and National Service, changed the rules so that women could now learn essential skills in Government Training Centres previously open only to unemployed men, but the centres were not a success. Also in 1941, the schedule of reserved occupations was scrapped. Block deferments in particular industries were replaced with individual deferments of key people.

Still the sums did not add up, but the Government remained reluctant to conscript women. Its natural inclination – and, especially, that of Bevin and Churchill – was to rely on volunteers. After all, even in Russia, Stalin did not direct women's involvement in the war effort on such a scale. Nor was this initial unwillingness confined to political circles: in 1939, London Transport had preferred to cut services rather than use women to fill its labour gaps.

One observer summed up the objections: the call-up of women would mean that 'Home life will vanish and it will be hard to revive after the war. Men coming home on leave will find they can only see their wives for an hour or two a day. Men in reserved occupations will come back to cold and untidy homes, with no meal ready. Friction in the home will be greatly increased and with children evacuated, there will be nothing to hold the family together.'

The Government persisted with official schemes to encourage volunteers, even though these sometimes did more harm than good. 'War Work Weeks', in 1941 and 1942 attracted hundreds rather than the thousands of volunteers hoped for. This was largely due to widespread resentment at the implication that a woman not in voluntary work was therefore shirking – always a poor basis on which to enlist cooperation and assistance. But if the conscription of women was a momentous step, it was also inevitable, and eventually the Government saw no alternative.

So for the first time, in late 1941, British women were conscripted. It was the only way the needs of the armed forces and essential war industries could be met, the nation fed, its cities defended and daily life in wartime organised effectively. Bevin had wide-ranging powers to direct and control the nation's workforce, and he had already taken control of wages and hours, largely with the support of the trade-union movement. The manpower budget was directly controlled by the Government.

At the beginning of December 1941, Parliament was told that all adults would be liable to be called up. On 18 December, the National Service (No. 2) Act came into effect. At first, the scheme was applied to women on a relatively small scale: only unmarried females between the ages of twenty and thirty were to be called up and they could choose whether to go into the auxiliary forces or into vital work in industry. It was also agreed that no women, whether in the civilian or military sphere, would be expected to fire a gun or bear arms of any kind.

By February 1942, all women aged between eighteen and sixty, married or single, with or without children, had to register with the Ministry of Labour. Even expectant mothers had to register, although they were exempt from work. Following registration, women were called for interview, according to age groups, to determine the sort of work each would do. Women already involved in important work or with children under fourteen living at home were the only ones not called at this point.

Those interviewed could volunteer for the auxiliary services, Civil Defence, the Land Army and the NAAFI (Navy, Army and Air Force Institutes) or could choose to work in a range of industries, including munitions, light alloys, timber production, post-office engineering, transport, vehicle maintenance and domestic work in hospitals, canteens and hostels for munitions workers. But compulsion was a fundamental part of the scheme in that just about every woman in Britain would be involved in officially sanctioned work. The term 'conscription' was applied to compulsory call-up to the auxiliary services; call-up to work in industry was commonly known as 'direction'. All eligible women could be directed into any civilian job and those who refused could be prosecuted, although the impracticalities of this measure soon became obvious, so prosecutions for refusing to take a civilian job were rare.

Volunteers were also dealt with in employment exchanges. Those already in work could volunteer for the auxiliary forces, for civilian work such as Civil Defence or for the Women's Land Army. Very soon it was decreed that women could be employed only through official (Government) labour exchanges. This came about because women directed initially into essential war jobs afterwards switched into less important posts, often for the same employer, for reasons which might be mutually convenient to employer and employee – but not to the Government.

As more women became involved, the need for flexibility to meet their concerns and requirements became equally obvious. To varying extents, these needs were met by employers. Care of children was a particular issue as mothers were given jobs. Crèches were established and local authority day nurseries sprang up. Part-time work, home-working, shift systems and special transport were introduced. Home workers were frequently depicted in local newspapers assembling aircraft parts on their dining room tables.

Children of working mothers in Maidstone are collected by nursery nurses in a lorry and taken to the day nursery. (Kent Messenger Group)

Very soon the scheme was in full swing. By the end of 1942, all women aged between eighteen and fifty had been registered and, unless she was involved in necessary war work or had children under the age of fourteen to look after, any woman between these ages would be called to the nearest employment exchange. At interview, domestic and financial circumstances were noted and the woman was given a choice of war occupations. Those accommodating soldiers or evacuees in their own homes also had this detail recorded.

The chief distinction between employing men and women was the issue of working away from home. Some work was reserved for women over thirty who were not able to leave

Women were interviewed for the type of war work they could do – voluntary, directed or conscripted – at their local employment exchanges. All men and women between the ages of eighteen and sixty-five had to register for war work. At first only a narrow band of women were called up. However, increasing manpower shortages meant that soon just about everyone had a job to do. (HMSO)

home. Many women had to stay within daily travelling distance, and they were referred to as 'immobile women'. Married women engaged in household work were defined as immobile, as were wives of men serving in the forces and the Merchant Navy. Men serving, especially those overseas, either took their wives with them or felt that moving wives out of their particular areas would break up their homes. The pressure from serving men, especially those in the Middle East, was such that 'many puzzled observers have often noticed . . . up and down the country, a certain number of young and healthy women, with no children and domestic duties, who appear to have so little to do' (*Man Power*, 1944). In general, older women were less mobile. They replaced usually younger single women who were moved around the country to do essential war work.

Those deemed 'mobile', might be sent just about anywhere. The country was divided into eleven regions, designated 'Supply' or 'Demand'. Demand Regions were linked to one or more Supply Regions. The idea was that mobile women in Supply Regions could be directed to other work in Demand Regions, even though this might sometimes mean they went from an essential role in one area to a not-so-essential role in another area.

Areas within regions were colour coded: scarlet areas were those in dire need of mobile unskilled women, where demand could not be met by that region's indigenous supply. Women had to be billeted in these areas from areas that were beyond normal daily travelling distances. Red areas were those where demand for unskilled women could be met only by retaining all the available women within their boundaries. There was no need for imported labour and no requirement to export their women. Amber was the code where supply and demand balanced but demand was not so urgent as red. This meant that some unskilled women in these areas could be directed to the 'screaming Scarlet areas'. Green areas were those in which anticipated demand could be met from existing labour and in which there should be available capacity. 'But if you come into the category of "surplus, unskilled mobile woman labour", it is ten to one that you will be moved out and given a travel warrant for one of the hammering, roaring Scarlets' the Government warned.

Equal pay was hardly an issue during wartime: an official survey found that for the vast majority of women, the money they earned was the major advantage of working but women did not see themselves as the main breadwinner. Those working in munitions, on the buses and on the railways were generally better paid than most, even though dif-ferent rates for men and women were applied.

Pay was an important distinction: by 1943, the average full-time weekly wage for a factory worker was £5 for men and £2 4s (£4.20) for women. The definition of 'full-time' differed for men and women too. The average working week for a man was 60 hours; for a woman, 55. Parliament voted that teachers, male or female, should all receive the same pay until Churchill got to hear of it. He vigorously opposed the idea, and the plan was ditched.

Employers were quick to see the financial advantages of employing women and the unions were equally quick to

This debate was all too common even in 1944, when this advertisement was published. This sort of publicity made it clear that whatever work women did, it was only a temporary arrangement to meet wartime needs.

see the pitfalls. As a result, concerted efforts to recruit women into the main unions resulted in a large increase in membership, but generally women who joined tended not to be active.

By mid-1943, almost 3 million married women and widows were in work, compared to 1,250,000 before the war. Almost 90 per cent of single women between the ages of eighteen and forty, and 80 per cent of married women were employed in the forces or in industry. Women made up one-third of the total workforce in metal and chemical industries, in ship-building and vehicle manufacture. The total number of women involved in all industries and the forces, excluding domestic service, was 7,750,000. Of these, about 750,000 worked part-time. Twice the proportion of women aged between fourteen and fifty-nine were employed in the forces, munitions and essential industries in mid-1943 as had been in 1918.

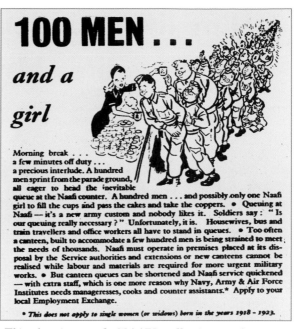

This advertisement, for NAAFI staff, points out that women aged between twenty-one and twenty-five cannot apply. They were needed for other work. The slogan is taken from an immensely popular 1937 Hollywood film of the same name. The original 'girl' was Deanna Durbin, a leading musical film star of the day, and the 100 men were unemployed musicians.

One year on, after D-Day in June 1944, the end of the war was in sight but production shortages persisted, as indeed shortages in many areas continued long after the war had ended.

In 1944, of 33,100,000 people in the country between fourteen and sixty-four, 17,200,000 were women; 4,500,000 women aged between eighteen and sixty-four were unmarried. Approximately 100,000 were involved in essential household duties. There were 9,000,000 children, almost entirely in the care of women. About 1,000,000 men and women aged over sixty-five were in paid employment. The newest recruits had to come from mainly married women with families, the last to be called up. A large proportion of these, about 840,000, worked part-time.

By the end of the war, women were encouraged to return to the home, releasing their jobs to men returning from active service. Home and family were the new preoccupations of the patriotic woman and pressure was on to conform by returning to this traditional role, in similar fashion to the end of the last war.

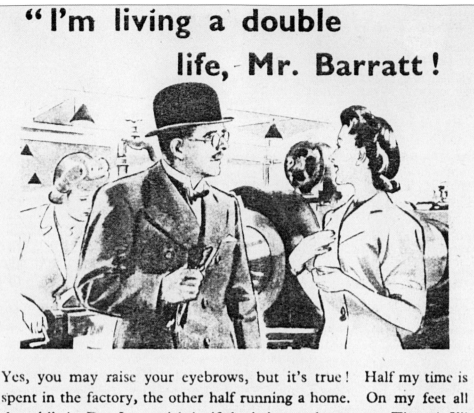

By 1944, when this advertisement appeared, the speaker would most likely have had that one pair of shoes for quite a while, too.

Wartime arrangements that had enabled women with families to work, such as flexible shifts and nurseries for young children, were withdrawn as no longer necessary. Single women were released from their wartime occupations. The Women's Land Army was one of the notable exceptions, as home food production had to be maintained.

So the vast majority of those who had worked during the conflict were now dismissed. Some were offered the chance to stay on, usually with lower wages and diminished status. Not surprisingly, most left, many preferring to start a family with their newly demobbed husbands.

CHAPTER 2

Civil Defence

Air raids in the First World War were scarcely worthy of being called this compared to those of the conflict twenty years later. During the First World War, aeroplanes, often operating alone, and the Zeppelin airships dropped bombs in a series of twenty raids over Britain between 1914 and January 1916. The following year, purpose-built bomber planes began raiding London. By the end of the war, 1,400 civilians had died in about 100 such attacks. Anti-aircraft guns, searchlights and air-raid warnings were all used but it was during the inter-war years that Civil Defence really began to develop.

Fears about the scale of devastation in any future conflict were grounded in two main beliefs: first, that gas, so feared in the trenches, would inevitably be used against civilians; secondly, that advances in aviation and bomb-making since the First World War would cause massive casualties in aerial bombardments.

Air-raid precautions were first discussed in 1924, by a specially convened sub-committee of the Committee for Imperial Defence. Nine years later, the ARP sub-committee decided that Civil Defence would be best placed under local authorities but little serious attention was paid to the matter. Then, in 1936, British cinemas showed graphic newsreel pictures of Guernica, the Basque town hit by German bombers supporting Franco's fascists in the Spanish Civil War. The public identified easily with the sufferings of people like themselves, and the devastation to streets very much like their own, and were horrified.

In January 1937, the first radio appeal for volunteers for ARP was broadcast across Britain. The response to this, like that of the local authorities charged with planning Civil Defence, was patchy.

So, in 1938, the ARP Act forced all local councils to draw up detailed schemes for Civil Defence, including plans for wardens, ambulance and first-aid services, and for expansion of the Fire Service. ARP provided messengers and wardens, an anti-gas service and decontamination and identification services. ARP also ran casualty services, first-aid parties and first-aid posts, stretcher parties and emergency ambulances. Women were volunteering in greater numbers than men.

Given the local nature of ARP, it was inevitable that variations in procedures and dress were common. But for most at this stage, an armband, a tin hat and a whistle were the nearest they had to a common uniform. Women were generally used in the ambulance service as drivers and assistants. In fact, many of the ambulance teams were entirely female. They ferried casualties to hospital during

A. R. P.
•
HOME OFFICE
SCOTTISH OFFICE
MARCH - - - - 1938

THIS leaflet sets out the choices open to every British citizen who wishes to take his or her part in the voluntary national organisation of the Air Raid Precautions Services.

As the Home Secretary said in his broadcast speech on the 14th March, 1938, " **If the emergency arose, I know you would come in your hundreds of thousands. But you would come untrained. For the work we may have to do one man trained beforehand is worth two or three who come at the last moment. We want at least a million men and women, and we want them for work that in an emergency would be exacting and dangerous. The job is not an amusement in peace-time, nor would it be a soft job in time of war. It is a serious job for free men and women who care for their fellows and for their Country.**"

The duties described here are mainly for what has been called passive defence. Young men preferring to take a part in the active defence of their country can enlist either in the Territorial Army (which provides the Anti-Aircraft Units for Home Defence) or in the Auxiliary Air Force; or in the Royal Navy (including the Royal Naval Volunteer Reserve) or Royal Marines, or the Army

It is not surprising that people expected a large-scale call-up of men and women, long before it was introduced by a reluctant government. This 1938 leaflet calls for 1 million men and women to volunteer for ARP (Air Raid Precautions).

and after raids in makeshift vehicles and transported non-urgent cases between hospital and home; they also took children to and from war nurseries.

In March 1938, the Government appealed for 1 million men and women to volunteer for ARP services, specifically to train as wardens. It drew little response. But when Hitler claimed for Germany the Sudetenland area of Czechoslovakia in September 1938, public opinion began to shift dramatically: for many people, the only question concerning the outbreak of war in Europe was when, not if, it would happen.

The British Government's lack of preparedness for, and reluctance to take, action led to the settlement known as the Munich Agreement – so-called because it was at Munich that Chamberlain, the British Prime Minister, and Hitler, as Chancellor of Germany, met with other European leaders. The result was the famous piece of paper that Neville Chamberlain held in his hand as he told the British people that 'peace for our time' had been achieved. Hitler incorporated the Sudetenland area into Germany and promised not to pursue further claims to any other part of Europe. The rest of Europe's leaders believed what they desperately wanted to believe.

Relief that war was no longer imminent was mixed, paradoxically, with the stark realisation that it was nevertheless inevitable. ARP accelerated with trial black-outs and practices involving all the services in imaginary incidents. The numbers of volunteers soared and even in areas where the threat had been largely ignored before, local authorities were busily putting together recruitment drives, appointing officers and setting up training schemes.

Terms and conditions for ARP workers were announced during 1939. The majority of people involved were expected to be part-time and the service to be essentially a volunteer force. Women working full-time in ARP were to be paid £2 a week; full-time male ARP workers were to be paid £3. Part-timers were also to be paid for time spent on call-out. Uniforms for both sexes were to comprise an armband and a tin hat, with special clothing and equipment for those dealing with gas.

Despite this upsurge in activity, however, Britain's ARP forces were still under strength when war finally broke out in September 1939. After the fear and frenetic activity that followed the Munich Crisis, people felt they had been misled about the likelihood and scale of the anticipated aerial bombardment. The eight months of what became known as the 'Phoney War' lasted until Dunkirk and the fall of France in May 1940.

ARP itself became a source of irritation and ridicule; wardens were popularly depicted as a group of busybodies who punctuated long hours playing cards and sleeping, with unwelcome visits to houses that showed a tiny chink of light, which was unlikely to guide even the lowest flying, non-existent bomber to its target. Nevertheless, preparations continued. As an emphatically civilian force, ARP members had no ranks. The jobs they did gave them authority only while they were doing them. In addition to the basic uniform, metal lapel badges and lettered tin helmets were the only indications of these roles. The first Government-issued ARP metal badge, designed by Eric Gill and produced by the Royal Mint, was in sterling silver and was given to everyone who had completed their training.

Ladies team of Canterbury Ambulance Depot, April 1940. Back row, left to right: Miss R. Woodward, Miss H. Pring, Miss B. Wilson. Front row: Miss R. Todd, Miss G. Hann. The FAP on Miss Wilson's helmet stands for First Aid Party. (Kent Messenger Group)

Soon, local authorities and private companies were issuing their own versions of Civil Defence badges. The local authorities issued the basic official badge free but those wearing them had to promise to pay for a replacement if it was lost, to surrender the badge on leaving the ARP service and not to give it to anyone else.

Nearly 1 million of these badges were in circulation before war broke out and, as uniform became more organised and extensive, they were usually worn as cap or lapel badges. Women's versions typically had a pin-back fixing and came in a blue box, whereas those for men were stud fastening and in red boxes. There were many variations. Some local authorities issued not just one, but a whole range of badges for various aspects of the service. Instructors, typically, had their own badges or the addition of a bar with the word 'instructor' on it. Factories and companies issued their own bearing the company name and, sometimes, trademark.

From late 1939, women were issued with mackintosh overall-type coats in bluette, a thin dark-blue denim material. The demands on ARP meant a more practical heavy battledress uniform was issued from 1941, consisting of a wool-type blouse, trousers, greatcoat and beret with the optional alternatives for women of skirt and ski cap or felt hat.

An ambulance driver with her vehicle, which followed Rescue Squads. Ambulance crews were trained in first aid, gas treatment and elementary mechanics. (HMSO)

Course No........2........   No.....151......

WORKSOP CORPORATION
ANTI-GAS SCHOOL

THIS IS TO CERTIFY that........Mrs. L. Cutler,..

...............................Sheffield Bank House, Worksop......................

has completed a course of Anti-Gas Training at this School and has acquired sufficient knowledge

of Anti-Gas measures to act as...a..member..of..the..Auxiliary..Nursing..section..in the Air Raid

Precautions Service.

Nature of Course attended..................Full Course.................

Instructor C.A.G.S..

Town Hall, Worksop

April 6th.......................1939 .   ... Town Clerk

ARP volunteers trained extensively in gas decontamination. Badges and certificates were awarded to those who completed courses. The date, April 1939, means that Mrs Cutler was one of the thousands who responded to the call for Civil Defence volunteers after the Munich Crisis of the autumn of 1938.

The early stages of the air assault were comparatively light: mainly single or small groups of aircraft attacking ships and coastal towns. It bore little resemblance to the feared Blitzkrieg. Ports and industrial areas, mainly in the south-east of England were the next focus of attention. In keeping with the usual tactics, German bombers and fighters sought to destroy the Royal Air Force, its pilots, planes and bases as a prelude to the invasion of Britain. The RAF and the Luftwaffe fought out the Battle of Britain but then, on 7 September 1940, the Nazi plan switched to mass bombing of London. ARP was suddenly the serious matter it had only intermittently seemed to be in the preceding years and months.

Alma Teague worked at the London Regional Civil Defence Headquarters, in the Geological Museum in South Kensington: 'I started just before the beginning of the war. I had my nineteenth birthday on 1st September 1939. A group of us worked at the Post Office Savings Bank – I found it very irksome – and I jumped at the chance of being able to work at regional HQ, which we were asked to do as our part in the National Emergency. We were all women, about 19, 20 years old. They divided into three shifts with 10–12 women on each, working 7am–3pm; 3–11pm; and 11pm–7am. We were in the hastily re-inforced basement. It was filthy – full of cement dust, rats and mice at first.' London was divided into nine areas and the job of headquarters' staff was to direct, plot and record what was happening with the various services across the capital during air raids. Alma Teague describes the early days:

> We did a lot of reading, knitting and played table tennis. We did any small jobs to keep ourselves occupied. In late 1939, we had a visit from King George and Queen Elizabeth so we spent ages cleaning the place. We managed to sweep the dirt out of the way and it was quite pleasant – the Queen even asked us how the air conditioning worked!
>
> We saw to the gas masks, checked the blackout, that sort of thing, but nothing really happened until after Dunkirk.
>
> They asked for volunteers for fire-watching and first-aid so I did that – anything for a laugh, we thought. I also liaised with the bomb-disposal group nearby.
>
> Then, on September 8th 1940, we had the first big raid on the London docks. My friend and I were upstairs and we opened the window in the ladies which was the only way we could hear and see it. Afterwards, there was a sense of 'is this what it's like?'

In her book *Raiders Overhead*, Barbara Nixon, a part-time warden in central London from May 1940, recalls the attitude of people in shelters during that first raid:

> No-one had any conception of what it was like. When the all–clear sounded at 6.15pm, people left the shelters saying 'about time too', little realising what was in store . . . I felt myself that that was to-day's raid . . . and went off to Soho for dinner that evening . . . I had not immediately grasped the principle that an important part of incendiary raids was to provide a beacon for later bombing. I was annoyed when the siren went again before we had even reached the coffee.

When we came out of the restaurant we stopped, aghast. The whole sky to the east was blazing red. The afternoon spectacle was completely dwarfed; it seemed as though half London must be burning . . . By 10pm the shelterers were growing exasperated; if it did not stop soon it would be past 'closing time'! By midnight they were frightened . . . I found that the bombs terrified me less than did the people in the shelters. It had not occurred to me before that a warden would be expected not only just to poke his head around the door to see if there was anything wrong, but to chat to one and all and try to cheer them up. In all the nine shelters that came within our province, I knew only two people slightly. I was horribly embarrassed.

The raid ended, as dawn broke and Barbara found people were cold, exhausted and subdued – as well as fearful that another such onslaught might come the following night. 'It was as well that they could not know that they were going to get "another" for fifty-seven nights on end, and after that, some raids were going to make this night's look like child's play.'

In 1940, in the London regional Civil Defence headquarters, Alma Teague moved to bombproof quarters, similar to the War Rooms in the Geological Museum's basement. 'Once the Blitz got underway, the raids would start about six o'clock in the evening and, as soon as the bombing started, public transport stopped. That had meant people on the 11pm shift had to get there before 6pm and if you finished at 11, it was difficult or impossible to get home. I was lucky in that I lived in Fulham, which was only a quarter of an hour away. One night, the raid started and I could not get into work. Then, at about 11.45, there was a sudden silence. So I grabbed my bike and, with my tin hat, my sandwiches and my knitting, I made a dash for it. But soon they altered our shifts to 8am–3pm and 3pm–8am, with the next day off. If the raids were not too bad and there was little enough to do, they would send some of us to have a rest on the camp beds upstairs.'

The CD headquarters had a telephone exchange, a message room and a control room. Essentially, its role of coordinating services across the nine London regions continued, albeit on a more urgent scale. Reports came in from all over London and the control office would direct ambulance, fire or other rescue services still on stand-by to the areas worst affected. Inevitably, HQ staff would take reports, plot and organise services sometimes to roads in which their own family and friends lived. Alma continues: 'Two of the girls lost their mothers in raids, but they just got on with the job – obviously you could not find out about particular people at the time. But the atmosphere was always one of calm during operations, at least. Staff knew they were safer than most of those under fire – had we taken a direct hit, we would have all died of concussion at least, but we knew very little about the raids in that basement.'

After the raids, squads would be called in to deal with unexploded bombs. Alma Teague helped make *UXB*, a training film for ARP: 'It talked about marshalling, evacuating homes and putting up barriers around a bomb. It was great fun to make.'

One of the smallest female Civil Defence services was the Women's Auxiliary Police Corps. At its height, it totalled no more than 10,000 members and their

The first female police officer at Waterloo.
(Kent Messenger Group)

duties were concerned with driving and administrative work. Unlike the Fire Service, the police never became a national force; this was reflected in the WAPC as each local group was attached to its county or city police force, with its own insignia and uniforms.

In 1939, men were to supplement the regular fire service by duplicating just about every aspect of the work of regular fire officers, but the official Government booklet, 'National Service', says vaguely that 'Women between the ages of 20 and 50 are wanted for appropriate duties.' The Women's Auxiliary Fire Service worked mainly in control centres and fire stations. From the outset, they operated switchboards and carried out clerical work. They also ran mobile canteens,

An early fire training exercise. The women's steel helmets are marked with the letters SFP – Street Fire Parties were the forerunners of the Fire Guard and dealt with incendiary bombs. (Kent Messenger Group)

drove tenders and other vehicles and were dispatch riders. Their roles here, as in many other areas, extended and developed as their abilities and the wider needs of the service were recognised.

Female pump crews became commonplace. However, Holcombe Fire Station in Chatham, Kent, was unusual in that it was run entirely by women. Once the work started in earnest, operational difficulties became apparent. Not least of these were the many variations in the sizes of hosepipes between counties, which often made the use of reinforcements from across county boundaries useless. Therefore, in August 1941, the National Fire Service was formed, and with it came largely successful attempts to standardise ranks, drill and, as far as possible, equipment.

Women had their own rank structure in the service: by 1943, the most senior

Two members of the Women's Auxiliary Fire Service repairing and maintaining the service's motor bikes and sidecars. (Catherine Gilman)

rank was Chief Woman Fire Officer. She wore epaulettes with three silver stripes alternating with red and topped by a small impeller; a cloth peaked cap with a single row of embroidered silver oak leaves, and a khaki steel helmet showing the NFS badge and three whiter stripes alternating with two narrower red stripes round the crown. The rank below this was Regional Woman Fire Officer, then Area Officer, Assistant Area Officer, Group Officer, Assistant Group Officer and Leading Firewoman.

It was far from being a quasi-military operation, however. Like their male colleagues, women in Civil Defence were proud of their volunteer origins and occasionally would exercise their right to cooperate or not with orders. In Bolton, for example, thirty NFS women walked out in protest at a new system that replaced 24-hour shifts with those of 48 hours. A meeting of the women voted not to cooperate with the new system, a spokeswoman afterwards emphasising, 'We are not deserting duty, we are merely operating the old system.'

Men and women shared many common details in their uniforms which were, after all, essentially practical for the jobs they were doing. Women's ceremonial dress consisted of tunic and skirt or trousers, cap, overcoat (at the discretion of the officer commanding), black shoes, steel helmet and respirator worn in the 'slung' position. When parading with men, women conformed with the style of male fire officers for respirators, steel helmets and so on.

WAFS Grotrian cleaning one of the brigade cars. Predicted demand for fire-fighting vehicles was such that anything capable of pulling a pump was likely to be called into service. (Catherine Gilman)

Marjorie Meath joined the AFS in 1940.

My husband was called up in September 1940 and I was left in our large flat. In November the flat was bombed and I was homeless so my mother-in-law, who lived in Darlaston, took me in and I travelled by bus and tram to Birmingham until it wore me out. So I applied to the AFS. Asked if I wanted administration or operational duties, I opted for the latter.

We were on 48/24 hour shifts (48 hours on/24 hours off) so on my day off, I slept at my mother's as she lived near to D Division HQ, where I was stationed.

First I learnt control duties, then switchboard. I was sent on an officers' training course but blew it because an officer said that there were only 23 hours 59 minutes in a day, not 24 hours. I argued, saying that I could not accept that if a fire call came through at midnight, I had to write it in the control book as 23.59 or 00.01. I said it would be a lie. So every month, when the divisional officer sent my name through for promotion it was that same officer who refused it. But I think I was happier on the ranks – they were such a wonderful crowd and there was such camaraderie between us.

Radio came in and two of us were sent for instruction and I loved that best of all duties. The DO would take me out in his car to measure the strength of the calls to central HQ. The idea was that if the calls to Central HQ were too weak, we would have to use dispatch riders for messages.

Then, one night, when we were all asleep in our bunks in the ladies dormitory, the sirens went. We all wore pyjamas so over the top of these went our jackets and trousers, then we scrambled down the fire escape into the control room to look at the list for who was on which duty. I settled down at the radio and gave our call sign. Then we waited and waited. The all-clear went finally and Central Control told us we could stand down. We were all shaking from being woken up so abruptly so when we returned to our bunks we couldn't sleep for the rest of the night. But off-duty, the next day, I slept right through to the evening through sheer exhaustion.

AFS women off duty early in the war. The AFS badges mean it is before the NFS was formed in 1941. Also there is a large amount of chocolate available on the table at the back. And only three out of the fifteen are knitting. (Catherine Gilman)

Marjorie Meath and her prize-winning pump team. Left to right: Eileen Hindley, 'Chick' Hood, Marjorie Meath and Jeannie Macpherson.

The crews were soon busy as raids stepped up, and training was extended so women could take on additional duties. Marjorie continues:

> When the raids eased off, the DO told four of us to train as a pump team as competitions were to be held for women. We did hydrant drills and pump drills each week at a fire station in Sutton Coldfield. We found the heavy hose hard work but as our muscles developed, it became easier. CO Perry was our trainer and as time went by, we became better and better, so when all the Midlands women's teams competed, our team won the cup. We took the cup round all our 11 stations and it was filled with something different at each one. Jeannie Macpherson and I just pretended to drink once we started feeling a bit squiffy but 'Chick' Hood and Eileen Hindley carried on drinking so they were drunk and Jeannie and I were just giggly. Next day we all had the inevitable headaches and swore 'never again'.

Civil Defence work meant bursts of frantic and non-stop activity for many, but for others air raids were largely a long-distance nuisance. Mary Archer was a teenager of sixteen when war broke out. Her parents took the Government's advice and moved from Finchley in north London to Oxford, away from the anticipated enemy action. Despite her pleadings to stay on at school, she had to leave and started work in the main branch of Lloyds bank in Oxford. 'In 1942, on becoming 18, I had to register for National Service so I joined Civil Defence. I learned first aid and was attached to a first aid post about two miles from my home. I had to sleep at the post on certain nights, but otherwise if the air raid siren blasted forth I cycled – with tin hat and CD respirator – to the post. The retired sister who was the Commandant said that before we even made our beds, we had first to put on the sterilisers because of injuries in the streets and women giving birth! Fortunately we weren't called on for either. But Oxford had a lot of air raid warnings as we were half way between London and Birmingham so we seemed forever on the alert.'

Fire-watching was introduced to cope with incendiary bombs. Edith Fox worked at the counter in the post office in North Street, Guildford, Surrey. 'The hours were 8.30am–6.30pm. Then we would go upstairs to do fire-watching all night. There would be three of us at a time and if the siren went off and we had to go to the shelter, I always made them wait while I put my corsets on – which caused great amusement.'

Mary Archer also did her share of fire-watching:

The idea of being in the services appealed to me – far better than the damp basement where we worked – but my job in the bank was considered more important so I was not called up. I could have volunteered but my parents were utterly opposed to this.

At the bank, we had to do fire-watching on a rota basis with the adjoining grocer's (either International Stores or Sainsbury's). We had some sort of instruction on dealing with incendiary bombs and I recall crawling around a fire in a disused building with the business end of a stirrup pump. Our training was never put to the test. We slept on camp beds in the attics but the breakfasts were great in the mornings as they were supplied by the grocers!

Kitty Goff, in Exeter, Devon, had more to do in the city's Civil Defence services:

Croydon ambulance driver Gwen Holland (left). One of the adapted saloon car's hooded headlights shows the letter A for Ambulance. 'I was on duty when Croydon airport was hit. A perfume factory was next to it and the smell of Evening in Paris hung in the air. I hated the smell for years after.'

Any vehicles that could be adapted were used as medical units, such as this one, pictured with some of its crew, which worked in the St Pancras area of London.

I was attached to the first aid team. Under the excellent teaching of Dr Charles Marshall, we took over Wrentham Hall in Prospect Park and converted it into a first aid post, not knowing from where the casualties were going to come. As soon as German aircraft came anywhere near, a loud siren sounded and we left whatever we were doing immediately to go to Wrentham Hall.

We attended Wrentham Hall, and Dr Marshall and the nurses gave us first aid lectures to try to make us as proficient as possible.

During the Blitz on Exeter, I was living some way up Pennsylvania Avenue, right down the road to the town. Bombs fell on Sidwell St and the High Street, including Bedford Circus where my father had his office, and the hospital. Stretcher cases were sometimes sent to us from the hospital and, being in a small building, they had to be put on the floor. In fact, if you went to the loo, it usually meant stepping over about five stretchers. The hall soon filled with casualties; we worked through the night. All the time, the atmosphere was one of complete calm.

When the bombers had gone, I stood out under the veranda and looked down towards the town: as far as I could see down the High Street and up Sidwell Street, it was a large sheet of flame – all the buildings were on fire and these were destroyed, including some of Southernhay.

One rule which generally held true throughout the war was the idea that whatever else women did, they should not bear arms. The Women's Home Defence League was one exception. Dr Edith Summerskill, MP for Fulham West, started this organisation in 1941.

The purpose of the league was to train women to assist the Home Guard by learning first aid, unarmed combat, morse code, field cooking and basic weapons skills. They were to be trained to fire a rifle but not to be issued with weapons. There was considerable pressure from women themselves to be allowed to join the Home Guard and carry weapons but this was resisted. Uniform was not encouraged, and WHDL members instead wore enamel badges with the league's initials and a crossed rifle. Within a year, over 200 WHDL units had been created.

'Dr Summerskill was of the opinion that if invasion did come, it was stupid for more than half the adult population of the country not to know how to use a rifle,' the *Kent Messenger* said on 30 January 1942, reporting on a local meeting calling for volunteers. 'Dr Summerskill pointed out that women could not pretend to take the same place as men in war. . . . She had been told by Home Guard commanders that they would use these women as messengers, for keeping open lines of communication, barricading and many other jobs, where a man could be spared to take on more active work.'

Lilian Coe was among the recruits who set up local branches of the WHDL.

Dr Summerskill held a meeting in Derby to recruit volunteers, and after her speech all the women started to leave, so I said, 'Why don't you take their names and addresses?', whereupon I was handed pen and paper, and thus became the organiser.

It was fun. I ran dances and whist drives to raise money for rifles (.22) and we were allowed 2,000 rounds of ammunition a month. We found three rifle ranges we were given permission to use, and an ex-army sergeant, Mr McGregor, gave us lessons in shooting, and also unarmed combat. Nurses from the infirmary taught us first aid, and the Home Guard taught us Morse code and field cooking.

Nanci Nicholls was in charge of St Pancras Medical Unit No. 1. An RFN (Registered Fever Nurse), SRN (State Registered Nurse) and SCM (State Certified Midwife), she had had to give up her job on marriage in April 1938. She was recalled because of the war, gave up in 1942 to have her first child, Susan, and then returned later because of the shortage of midwives.

Some men thought we were a joke, but we soon disillusioned them. One office wallah was downright rude, and we had a lovely little slim girl who was good at unarmed combat. She said very sweetly, 'You can't offend me Les, so shake hands to prove there is no ill feeling.' The next moment he was flat on his back. He said, 'You couldn't do that if I was prepared.' She agreed and offered her hand again in apology. Again he landed flat on his back, and no more rude jibes were made. Another time, we challenged a group of the Home Guard to a shooting match and beat them hands down.

As time went by, the vast majority of the league's members went into the Home Guard, as non–combatants. In April 1943 they were officially allowed to join the

*These two first-aid
post workers in
Springfield, Essex,
wear nursing overalls
in blue and white
pinstripe, with the
letters ARP in red.*
(Imperial War
Museum)

Home Guard, and were known as 'nominated women' until they were renamed
Home Guard Auxiliaries in July 1944. By the end of the war, they totalled
30,000 members. Many wore battledress or other uniform, although this was not
officially issued. Home Guard Auxiliaries could wear a special plastic badge on
the left side of a coat or dress although uniformed units preferred to wear it as a
cap badge. Certificates issued to Home Guard Auxiliaries recognised them as
eligible for protection under the Geneva Convention. The WHDL continued
until 1944, when it metamorphosed into the Women's Rifle Association, which
continued after the war.

After a flurry of activity during the Blitz, the work of Civil Defence volunteers
generally quietened down until 1944, with the arrival of the new threat posed by
V1s and V2s, which flattened entire streets. In 1944, Olive Owens (née
Stevenson), aged 17, was one of the youngest air-raid wardens in the country. She
worked a 10-hour shift each weekday before going on duty as a warden.

I was based in the cemetery in Bonner Hill Road in Croydon and one of my duties was to walk the cemetery looking for incendiary bombs. I also had a spell of duty in the underground shelters underneath the Fairfield.

One day when I was on duty, a V2 rocket dropped on the corner of Park Road and King's Road. It was complete devastation. We dug and dug until our fingers bled.

My most vivid memory is of an arm raised, to call for silence, when someone heard tapping among the ruins.

The American Red Cross was very good at keeping us in doughnuts and American coffee and I also remember well the astonishment of one American Sergeant when he realised how young I was to be doing that job and working full-time elsewhere too – but it was nothing in those days. Everyone did it.

Olive Owens (née Stevenson), aged seventeen, one of the youngest ARP wardens in the country in 1944.

Girls too young to join ARP could still play their part through established national organisations such as the Girl Guides Association, or local groups such as the Girl's Emergency Administration Service, based in Dartford, Kent. Girls would visit wounded soldiers in hospital, taking small gifts or writing letters for those too badly injured to do it themselves. Margaret Peers, herself aged about fourteen at the time, recalls the hospital ships as they docked in Liverpool: 'We would greet the injured soldiers and promise that we would visit them in hospital to make sure they were all right.'

It was a feature generally of women's involvement in the war effort that women themselves were sometimes way ahead of Government bodies in their enthusiasm to get involved. The Women's Junior Air Corps was, like the Women's Home Defence League, one of many examples of this. At the end of 1939, the National Youth Committee was working with local youth groups to train and support young people helping in the war effort. The Government appealed for volunteers to work as youth leaders. One who responded was Enid Walter, who set up the Women's Air Cadet Corps, renamed (at the request of the Air Ministry) the Women's Junior Air Corps. It provided basic training and social activities for girls between the ages of fourteen and seventeen. The Air Ministry refused it official recognition, and even banned units of the RAF and Air Training Corps from parading with it. But by 1942, it had 20,000 members in 212 units, most of them based in the north of England.

Margaret Peers aged sixteen. Girls like Margaret were too young for ARP duties but worked as volunteers in hospitals which received injured soldiers.

A naval equivalent, the Girls' Naval Training Corps, was founded in 1942 by Commander C.L.A. Wollard, a retired naval officer. It was totally independent of the Admiralty until 1945, when it was officially sanctioned only after its leaders agreed to the name being changed to the Girls Nautical Training Corps.

The Girls Training Corps was another unofficial organisation equally as unpopular with the Government as it was popular with girls wanting to 'do their bit'. Its origins were in the Mechanised Transport Corps, although other groups taking the GTC name were set up independently. By the time the Government stepped in to curb this proliferation of enthusiastic and, as far as it was concerned, uncontrollable organisations, the GTC had 799 units in a wide range of settings, including girls' boarding schools such as Cheltenham Ladies College and in London boroughs.

So, in 1942, the Government announced that no more companies of the WJAC, units of the GNTC, GTC or other similarly unofficial bodies could be formed. Instead, the Board of Education set up a coordinating body to oversee all training groups for girls in the WJAC and the GTC. In this new body, the National Association of Girls' Training Corps, all new units were to be known only as GTC companies. Each member had to provide her own uniform comprising a skirt, blouse and tie, with a side cap and a dark-blue jacket for officers. Ranks were denoted with various types of pin badges. The Junior GTC was open to those under sixteen and they wore a variation on the uniform for older members of the corps. Despite the attempts to control all such groups for girls under this national association, other local groups were formed and carried on throughout the war.

After the end of hostilities, in late 1945, the naval and air groups became independent and officially recognised bodies, continuing into the post-war era, as did the National Association of Training Corps for Girls. ARP, its work over, was stood down on 2 May 1945, as were women who had joined the NFS. ARP no longer had a job to do and women who had joined the Fire Service were auxiliaries who had signed up only for the duration of the war.

CHAPTER 3
Women's Voluntary Services

Women's Voluntary Services were an early success story in Civil Defence. Established in 1938 by Stella Isaacs, the Dowager Marchioness of Reading, it grew quickly out of arrangements set out in the Air Raid Precautions Act which came into effect on 1 January 1938, by which time Lady Reading was already holding first-aid and gas defence classes at her home in Chesterfield Street, London. Born in 1894, she was experienced in voluntary service and, until their marriage in 1931, worked as secretary to the Marquess of Reading, former viceroy of India and ambassador to the USA. She was a close friend of Eleanor Roosevelt, the wife of the then American President. The two women shared a deep

Stella Isaacs, Dowager Marchioness of Reading, who founded the WVS, interviews three new recruits. It must be early days as they have all brought their gas masks.

commitment to alleviating poverty and Lady Reading's approach was both practical and persuasive. During the depression, she had set up the Personal Service League, a national voluntary organisation that provided clothing for unemployed men and their families – a useful forerunner of the clothing schemes run by the WVS (as it was known) during the war that recycled, particularly, children's clothing that had been outgrown.

The arrangements for ARP schemes were outlined in the 1938 pamphlet 'What You Can Do' and, when taking the view that more women than men volunteered, the Home Secretary asked Lady Reading to draw up a proposal for an organisation of women in ARP. Lady Reading, on the other hand, felt that far too few women had volunteered. Worse, in the absence of any clear roles or duties, those who had offered to help had soon drifted away. She wrote a memorandum that set out an extensive scheme for a wide-ranging voluntary organisation. She wanted an advisory council, which would represent all the main women's voluntary organisations in the country, and a small executive committee; regional offices would work with local authorities, who would be responsible for training and local branches of the new organisation would provide clerical and other support. Minimal expenses would be paid to a very small minority. Lady Reading also identified key people she felt would form an efficient and well-organised headquarters' staff, which she viewed as essential to deal with a vast number of enthusiastic but untrained volunteers.

On 16 May, Sir Samuel Hoare held a confidential meeting at the Home Office to discuss the formation of the WVS. Subsequently, he set out the objectives of the organisation as 'the enrolment of women for Air Raid Precautions Services of Local Authorities, to help to bring home to every household what air attack may mean, and to make known to every household in the country what it can do to protect itself and the community'. At the end of May, an informal, confidential meeting of representatives of women's organisations, chaired by Lady Reading, was held in London. Most of those present promised support for the advisory council of the WVS. A similarly successful meeting in Scotland was chaired by Lady Ruth Balfour.

Inevitably, there were arguments between the various organisations and those who believed, with the benefit of experience, that cooperation between them would be, in the words of one observer, 'a hopeless business'. Lady Reading herself is frequently described as 'charismatic' and this, with her commitment, organisational powers and extensive contacts, was crucial in getting the scheme off the ground.

As with many other civilian and forces organisations of women established at this time, the WVS relied for its speedy development on the existing class system for both the structure and contacts it needed. *Green Sleeves*, the official history of the WVS, records that Lady Reading's 'team of friends' included Priscilla Norman, the wife of the governor of the Bank of England, who became the Vice-chairperson of the WVS, and Mrs Lindsay Huxley, the Honorary Treasurer of the National Federation of Women's Institutes, who became Chief Regional Administrator, as well as people from the Personal Service League. Other key positions were filled through personal contacts and unofficial links set up with leading members of other movements such as the Girl Guides.

This poster is one of the first from the WVS so it emphasises the service's role in ARP. (HMSO)

Books were in demand both as salvage to meet the demand for scarce paper and to stock libraries for servicemen. The Mammoth Paint Book, *held by the woman third from the right, is probably going to be pulped.*

The WVS dealt with the nitty-gritty of setting up an organisation and defining its role against this background of urgency. Its ethos, like that of ARP in general, was of an emphatically voluntary organisation, so no individual held rank. The chain of command was instead based around tasks that needed to be done and Lady Reading regularly commented 'It's the job that counts'. This meant, for example, that a woman in charge of a salvage collection had the authority to organise others from the WVS for that purpose. If she moved somewhere else, she would relinquish that authority to the person taking over that task.

Also in the early stages, it was established that WVS members were not expected to raise money and discipline was a personal or local matter. A vast range of training courses was soon organised. These included driving in the black-out; child care, with the help of the National Council for Maternity and Child Welfare; and courses to provide trainers for local authorities. In London, this instruction was given in Italian, French, Spanish, Dutch and Yiddish for foreign nationals.

The WVS uniform was another issue, largely resolved at this time. The only colour available was green, initially rejected by other civilian defence

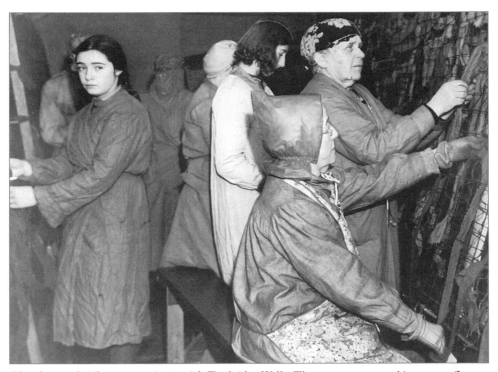

Not the usual sight one associates with Tunbridge Wells. These women are making camouflage nets, one of the major activities organised and co-ordinated by all the voluntary services. (Kent Messenger Group)

forces on superstitious grounds. To overcome this, the twill cloth was woven in grey and green. The blouse, like the lining of the overcoat, was dark red and a beret or felt hat completed the ensemble. The well-cut, dressy appearance was due to its designer, Digby Morton, a Dublin-born couturier working in London for the Paris house of Lachasse, who had become well known during the 1930s for his severe and stylish suits. The uniform was not compulsory nor free. Many WVS members wore just the service's silver and red lapel badges, initially bearing the letters ARP under the King's Crown and the legend 'Women's Voluntary Services'. As the WVS remit was extended, the badge was amended with WVS in red above the words, 'civil defence'.

Meetings calling for volunteers and explaining the work of the WVS were arranged, especially in cities where air attack was thought most likely. Major voluntary organisations were involved, including the British Red Cross Society, the Charity Organisation Society (now known as the Family Welfare Association) and St John Ambulance. Training was organised and called for by the WVS but it was provided by bodies such as the St John Ambulance Brigade and Red Cross, who were recognised by the Home Office.

WVS County Evacuation Officers were appointed as the first major task of the WVS was the evacuation of children and, in some cases, their mothers, from areas of high risk in the weeks following the Munich Crisis of September 1938. Within 36 hours, the WVS had organised itself so that if bombing started, a quarter of a million women would be ready for action under the direction of local leaders. In the essentially improvisational world of passive defence, the Government learned a great deal, even though the evacuation was called off before many children had been transferred to safer places. The major lesson was that Britain was totally unprepared, although the WVS was seen as something of an exception.

Immediately, the WVS was asked to carry out a national billeting survey and the service also worked closely with the Evacuation Department set up by the Ministry of Health. Twelve regional organisers were appointed across the country. By the beginning of 1939, the WVS was established as the official channel for recruiting women to Civil Defence services.

A second evacuation, at the end of August 1939, had also been a learning experience. Not least because of the discrepancy between the generally well-organised arrangements for departure from dangerous areas and the more chaotic situation on arrival at safe havens.

Many trains were diverted, or delayed, to allow scheduled trains to pass. Even those trains that arrived as expected had quite often set off with their destinations unknown. People expected to report to the assembly points for evacuation did not arrive, having made their own plans instead. Those arriving as expected were put on the first available train. As a result, some safe areas were ready to receive many more evacuees than actually arrived while others were overwhelmed. Many local authorities gave responsibility and powers for billeting to the WVS. Members prepared billets for children and instead received pregnant mothers.

Another important lesson was the effect of holding this evacuation during the school holidays: it meant that routine medical examinations were not part of the plan so those with lice or fleas or scabies were not identified and treated. Instead, even where the stays were brief, many took the newly acquired parasites back to their homes. WVS members in reception areas responded by de-lousing, writing pamphlets and giving lectures on dealing with infestation.

Despite these hiccoughs, however, in those few days before war was formally declared on Sunday 3 September 1939, the WVS organised the removal of nearly 1½ million people, mainly children, from areas at risk from the poison gas and bombs which, it was thought, would inevitably be falling on major cities and ports as soon as hostilities commenced. It was at this time that the then Queen Elizabeth, now the Queen Mother, became the WVS President.

Billeting and transport aside, clothing was a major issue for the service. Lady Reading broadcast an appeal to the USA in October 1939, detailing the WVS role in the evacuation scheme. She talked about the knitting and sewing circles, the canteens to give evacuees a hot meal and the need for warm clothing for the coming winter.

The response was overwhelming and stockpiles of clothing, blankets and other items flooded in via the American Red Cross. They came initially to the Personal Service League, in which Lady Reading no longer had an official role. There were concerns that American neutrality would be affected if the supplies were sent directly to the WVS. These 'Bundles for Britain' were later sent direct to the WVS as American involvement on the side of the Allies became a reality. During the Blitz, in the second half of 1940, £1½ million worth of clothing, mainly from the USA, Canada and the Commonwealth, had arrived for distribution by the WVS from its Emergency Clothing Stores.

The supplies were soon needed. Refugees from the Continent fled across the Channel and were billeted through local War Refugee committees working closely with the WVS. Most arrived with only the clothes they stood up in, including some from the Channel Islands who arrived wearing just their bathing costumes.

Internment of enemy aliens was stepped up in June 1940 as the threat of invasion loomed and the WVS, as in other areas, helped with sandwiches, tea and transfers of those who were to be interned. But the next major crisis was Dunkirk. Between 26 May and 4 June 1940, 338,682 members of the British and Allied forces were lifted from the beaches of Dunkirk in Operation Dynamo.

The WVS greeted the troops on arrival at ports all around the south coast of England. They provided hot tea, snacks, cigarettes and warm, dry clothing. They took messages for families, darned and washed socks – and even the men wearing them – before the troop trains went on to their eventual destinations. Trains carrying hundreds of men, arriving at intervals of about 20 minutes at stations throughout the country, would each be met with supplies. One of the busiest stations was at Headcorn in Kent, where trains would draw up for an 8-minute food stop on their journey. Women cut thousands of sandwiches each day, working round the clock in shifts; beef was roasted on open spits and thousands of pies, sausages, eggs and rolls were served up daily. From all over the country, WVS members sent clothing and toiletries from the stocks collected. They set up rosters of cycle messengers and drivers, and hostels for relatives of casualties, as local conditions required.

When the soldiers had left the south of England, refugees arriving from Gibraltar and the Channel Islands were billeted in these hostels. By now, volunteers were adept at running mobile canteens and finding places for displaced people to stay. But the scale and pace, if hectic up to now, was as nothing compared to the next phase of the war. In September 1940, the Luftwaffe began bombing London and other major cities in the United Kingdom. The Blitz had begun.

A feature of the Civil Defence and especially the WVS, was its ability to take up quickly a successful local initiative and apply it nationally. Many women were willing to volunteer but could not leave their homes in times of emergency. The WVS in Barnes, west London, formed a Housewives Service in response to the problem. The official history records that when the local ARP officer asked the local branch of the WVS to do this, the head of the WVS Technical Department observed that 'the idea was mainly of keeping WVS out of mischief and he probably never envisaged a time when the Barnes Housewives Service would be an integral part of the Borough Civil Defence Scheme'. The technical officer soon found herself in charge of thousands of housewife volunteers and similar schemes were set up all over the country.

This card, in blue, white and black, would be displayed in a window of the home of a member of the service.

Volunteers for the Housewives Service worked from home so they were issued with cards to put in their windows. Many wore a WVS armlet or badge. Their duties centred around assisting local wardens after an air raid. Typically, they would supply cups of tea to casualties and workers, look after elderly people and give immediate and temporary shelter to people whose houses had been bombed. They received training in first aid and anti-gas measures, and helped with updating the Household Register, which gave house by house information on the occupants and layout of each inhabited place in an area. By 1943, many had also been trained in fire-guard duties.

No one expected the Blitz to go on for long. London was bombed for fifty-seven consecutive nights and although the majority of those made homeless made alternative arrangements themselves, the WVS found itself coping with many times more than the 10,000 each night it had envisaged would attend the rest centres organised for families whose homes had been damaged or destroyed.

The main problem was that, in theory, the rest centres were generally expected to house families for a few hours or, at most, one night, while other accommodation was sought. In practice, people stayed for weeks. Also, rest centres were organised under Public Assistance schemes and so ran within the rigid and even archaic structure of the Poor Laws. There was little room for improvisation as red tape and the variable abilities of local authorities to cope with reality dominated provision. In London, 6 weeks into the bombing campaign,

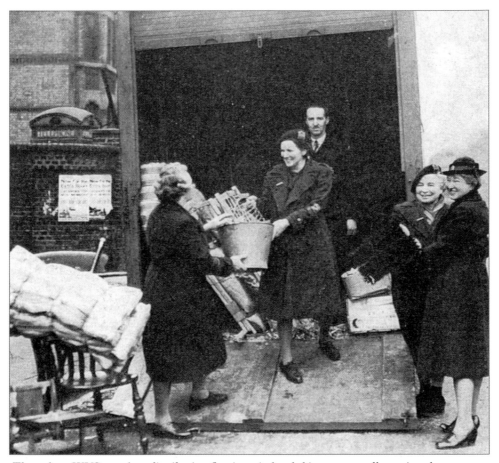

These three WVS members distributing furniture in bomb-hit areas are all wearing the overcoats designed by Digby Morton. The two on the left are wearing the WVS beret with grey cloth badge and red embroidery, while the woman on the right is wearing the WVS trilby with metal pin-on badge.

with 250,000 people homeless, rest centres housed 25,000. Local authorities were slow to organise rehousing: only 7,000 had been found somewhere else to live.

Rest centres were established in church halls, schools and similar buildings, often hurriedly and often with minimal facilities. Sanitation, food and other basics were initially conspicuous by their absence. The WVS' flexibility meant it could respond to varying needs on the ground, and its national structure meant training of volunteers and distribution of supplies could be organised effectively.

The service continued to provide clothing, food, blankets and other items to families whose homes had been damaged. Lectures and pamphlets aimed at members and the general public gave advice on coping with the latest crisis. Members had to hand out a range of practical pamphlets that included such titles as 'What shall I do before going to the shelter?' and 'Behaviour and advice for shelter users'. The mobile canteens and rest centres, almost entirely staffed by WVS volunteers, were fully stretched.

Towards the end of 1940, the London County Council asked the WVS to carry out a survey of second- and third-line rest centres. Rest centres were defined as first, second or third line according to their relative proximity to the area bombed, the first-line centres being the nearest. The LCC took over about a hundred of the second- and third-line centres, bringing them up to the standards of those designated first-line rest centres. The WVS was asked then to take over the remaining centres and was promised supplies from County Hall for essentials. Communal feeding centres were established. In Barnes, one WVS member fed 1,200 people from her own kitchen the day after a night-time raid. Members showed people how to build crude brick ovens in the street. During raids, mobile canteens brought tea and sandwiches to those in shelters and to ARP workers fire-fighting, rescuing buried casualties and dealing with dangerous buildings.

Inevitably, there were casualties: 241 WVS members were killed during the bombing and many more injured. By May 1941, twenty-five WVS offices had been destroyed and the service had learned the necessity of keeping duplicate records at locations distant from vulnerable places. Like most Civil Defence services, its reputation grew throughout the war.

Lady Reading and Mrs Thompson seen in the bomb-damaged WVS centre in Sturry, Kent. Lady Reading has the WVS badge on her bag. Mrs Thompson and other local volunteers were looking after Allied servicemen when their centre was hit. Lady Reading wears the armband of senior Civil Defence officers. (Kent Messenger Group)

Most lorries were driven by men, but the Queen's Messenger Food Convoys were otherwise composed of women who brought hot food to areas badly hit by bombing. (HMSO)

One problem that hampered ARP rescue workers in the early stages was that of anxious relatives asking for news of their families. Incident Inquiry Points were established near to affected areas to deal with these queries. IIPs were marked at first with a poster designed by the WVS and were set up in houses, shops or even simply with tables in the street. Initially run by ARP rescuers, the WVS took over this role to release ARP teams.

When a tip-and-run raider bombed Sandhurst Road school in Catford, south London, in January 1943, members of the WVS accompanied parents through the wreckage and took down details identifying the children killed and injured. The service was officially asked to take on this aspect of post-raid work shortly afterwards and training was begun. In autumn 1943 the first WVS-run IIP was opened at St Pancras in London. The following year, preparation complete, the service took over all responsibility for IIPs from ARP.

Bombing raids created another problem that needed to be resolved in the immediate aftermath: local services simply could not cope with the demand for food from a homeless population. The answer was the Queen's Messenger Food Convoys. Named after the then Queen Elizabeth, who donated the first of eighteen such services – the remainder were mainly provided by the USA – these convoys would set off for areas that had suffered heavy raids. As many vehicles as could be commandeered were loaded up with food and water with women called out at short notice to staff them. The convoy would travel to a safe town nearest to the affected area and stay there for several days, feeding thousands of people. Men would drive the heavy vehicles but otherwise the convoys were run entirely by women of the WVS.

The first convoy, which left Lewisham, south London, in November 1940, was sent to help the people of Coventry during the raids that devastated the city. Four motor cyclists and eight lorries accompanied by twenty-seven staff travelled the 100 miles in just under 5 hours. Many women had left their homes so quickly that their husbands and children returned home later in the day to find a hastily scribbled note – and no indication of when the women would be back.

The convoy stayed overnight in a children's home in a nearby town, rather than risk being caught in another raid as evening fell. At 7 a.m. next morning, it entered the ravaged city. The WVS was soon distributing soup, sandwiches and tea as rescuers worked and delayed action bombs exploded around them. By the time they left two days later, the first Queen's Messenger Convoy had served 14,000 meals to the citizens of Coventry. As ever, lessons were learned and acted upon, not least that centres that were vulnerable to attack needed reserve teams standing by.

The prevailing attitude of the WVS was summed up by one member in Coventry in Humphrey Jennings' 1941 film, *The Heart of Britain*: 'You know, you feel such fools, standing there in the crater, holding up mugs of tea while the men bring up bodies. You feel so useless until you know that there is someone there, in that bombed house who is alive, and who you can actually give that tea to. Then to have the praises of the men themselves: "that tea is jolly good. It washed the blood and dust out of my mouth." And we feel that we really have done the job – and a useful job.'

By 1941, over 1 million women were enrolled in the WVS and many of them were involved in organising the collection of salvage throughout the country. The Housewives Service in particular had developed during the bombing and by 1942, when it was renamed the Housewives Section, it comprised 20 per cent of the entire service.

As the Blitz came to an end, a more long lasting and widespread problem was looming, in which the WVS would play a major part: shortages began to bite as the Battle for the Atlantic was fought. The response on the Home Front was salvage reclamation on a scale that would put to shame the peacetime recycling schemes of the late twentieth century.

The salvage drives were enthusiastically taken up by children and adults alike and the service coordinated efforts to collect wastepaper, wool, food for pig-swill and, most famously, scrap metal. The drive to donate metal was the idea of Lord Beaverbrook. Everything from saucepans to the railings from municipal parks was gathered. Unfortunately, the metal concerned was of no use whatsoever for making Spitfires and Hurricanes but this was glossed over by the authorities who took the view that the collection at least had the effect of maintaining morale.

Each centre had its own salvage officer whose job was to keep up enthusiasm for the innumerable schemes. Street collection points were set up with bins labelled 'bones', 'paper' or 'pig food'. Parties were arranged with the theme of 'Make Do and Mend' and schemes specifically for local schools were created. Roger Campion recalls:

My mother helped organise the local knitting circle which comprised about ten ladies. These ladies undertook the knitting of scarves, balaclavas, gloves and socks for the army or air force. Once each week they would come to our house to bring the items they had completed since their last visit, have a cup of tea, do some knitting and have a chat.

A few of the ladies had children under school age and they would come along with their mums. This was fine except that no matter how I tried to hide my toys either the children or my Mum found them. Early in 1940, my parents bought me the last set of lead soldiers in our town. They were very dear to me – a group of Scots Greys in full regimental dress with swords drawn, mounted on the famous grey horses. Before long, the soldiers' heads were broken off to be repaired with matchsticks! Rubber tyres from Dinky toys were scattered everywhere, clockwork motors overwound. However, as my Mother pointed out, it kept them quiet.

Every few weeks someone would come and collect the completed items and deliver fresh supplies of knitting wools. A strict check was kept on the quantities of wool supplied and woollens collected – so I didn't get any spare socks or gloves.

My mother received the standard certificate acknowledging her efforts and expressing the government's thanks.

The local nature of many initiatives disguised the enormous scale of the work: when clothes rationing was introduced in 1941, the WVS Clothing Exchange had to unpack, measure and give a coupon assessment to its entire stock – over £5 million worth of clothing. When the Government brought in food rationing, the service organised the distribution of 45 million ration books and followed this up, inevitably, with lectures and pamphlets on making the best of available resources. Food Leaders were created to oversee many of the numerous local schemes and services.

Fundraising for war supplies was an important feature of daily life. Campaigns such as Salute the Soldier, Spitfire Funds, Wings for Victory and Warship Weeks were held when towns and cities bought their own battleship or Spitfire. Peter Good remembers one scheme organised in Derby: 'A collection was made weekly towards the provision of a War Memorial Village in which those who had been disabled by their injuries might live in comfort. It sounds incredible but volunteers were enrolled to visit a particular street on a weekly basis, collecting a penny from each household to raise the necessary cash for this. On a Thursday, for a number of years, my mother was one such collector – they had record cards to mark and each week their takings had to be passed on to a central collector. I am sure this little job only took about an hour a week, but the War Memorial Village was built and the houses still stand today.'

W·V·S CIVIL DEFENCE

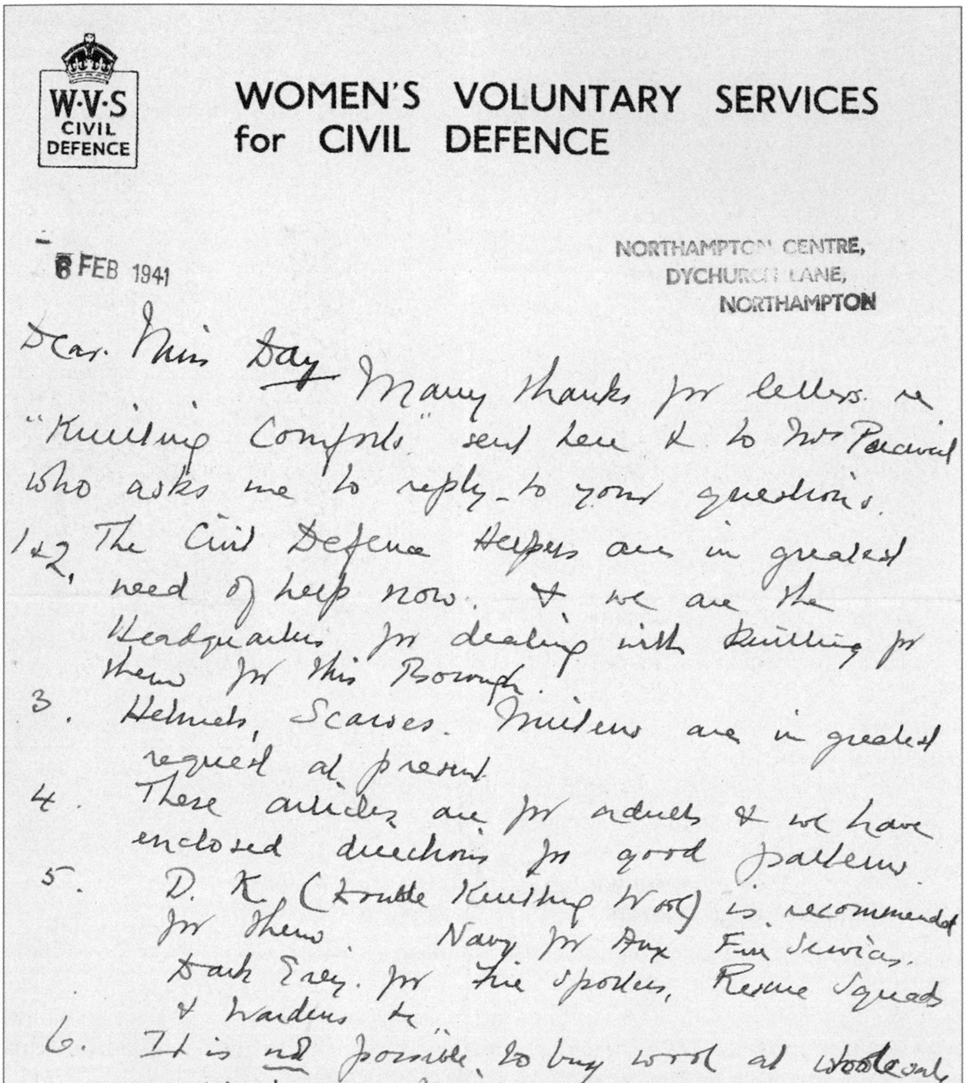

WOMEN'S VOLUNTARY SERVICES for CIVIL DEFENCE

8 FEB 1941

NORTHAMPTON CENTRE,
DYCHURCH LANE,
NORTHAMPTON

Dear Miss Day

Many thanks for letters re "Knitting Comforts" sent here & to Mrs Percival who asks me to reply to your questions.

1 & 2. The Civil Defence Helpers are in greatest need of help now. & we are the Headquarters for dealing with knitting for them for this Borough.

3. Helmets, Scarves. Mittens are in greatest request at present.

4. These articles are for adults & we have enclosed directions for good patterns.

5. D. K. (Double Knitting Wool) is recommended for them. Navy for Aux Fire Services. Dark Grey. for Fire Spotters, Rescue Squads & Wardens &c.

6. It is not possible to buy wool at wholesale or reduced prices.

Thanking you for your kind offer

Yours sincerely

Alice. E. Chapman

Joint Sec

Alice Chapman, joint secretary of the Northampton Centre, writes to Miss Day, answering her numbered queries about knitted comforts. '1 & 2. The civil defence workers are in greatest need now and we are the headquarters for dealing with knitting for them for this borough . . . 6. It is not possible to buy wool at wholesale or reduced prices.' Well, this is 1941.

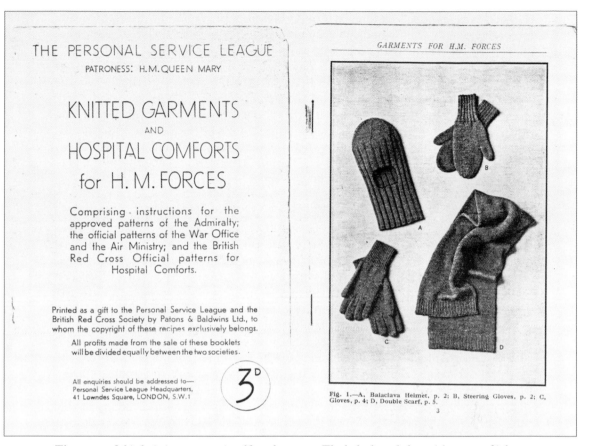

The cover of this knitting pattern is self-explanatory. The balaclava helmet (A on page 3) has the smallest possible gap for the eyes.

As usual, local needs stimulated ideas that were then taken up across the country. The Rural Pie Scheme was one such inspiration. In late 1941, Cambridge WVS workers supplied those in the fields at harvest time daily with hot meat pies. Over 70,000 pies were cooked and distributed and by the end of the year, the Ministry of Food was instructing local authorities on establishing similar schemes, provided by commercial catering firms. Petrol rationing meant that those who had been able to volunteer their vehicles as well as themselves could no longer form the WVS transport services. Instead, the Ministry of Home Security set up the Volunteer Car Pool scheme, basing it on the WVS scheme. By the end of 1942, titles, jobs and badges had broadened to take into account this extended range of duties. But, as before, the essentially volunteer nature, with its absence of official ranks of the service, prevailed.

Later, when heavy bombing raids had been replaced by the V1 and V2 rockets, Food Convoys were replaced by Food Flying Squads. In 1944, a scheme for Food

Leaders was launched nationally. The 15,000 leaders appointed in the following year were mainly from among WVS housewives. Their task was public education and advice on making the best of food as shortages increased.

As the raids continued, all WVS members were asked to volunteer for basic Civil Defence training. Here, as in other areas, their main function was to be ready to fill in any gaps that could not be taken up by other agencies.

As hundreds of thousands of British and Allied forces massed in preparation for the invasion of France on D-Day, a popular joke at the time was that it was only the barrage balloons that prevented the south coast of England from sinking under the weight of troops and equipment. Plugging the gaps as D-Day approached was an enormous task for the WVS, which, by the end of 1943, had over 1 million members.

Mobile canteens and other facilities met and supplied the troops at ports and railway stations around the country just as they had during the evacuation from Dunkirk. Libraries were set up wherever there were gaps in the facilities offered by other agencies and thousands of WVS members were placed in forces hospitals. Welcome clubs were set up for incoming troops. An unforeseen problem arose with American GIs in that their troops were emphatically segregated. So the service obligingly established two clubs for USA army personnel in Piccadilly – one for 'white' and one for 'coloured' GIs.

As D-Day approached, WVS members were out in strength around the south and east coasts of England, distributing snacks and other comforts to British and other Allied troops, often by torchlight and always sworn to the utmost secrecy about what they had seen and where. Canteens continued their work in the docks, supporting dockers who toiled at breakneck speed unloading ships bringing in vital supplies. Lorry drivers were helped along their way with special WVS rest centres.

V1s and V2s, the first a pilotless aircraft and the second a fully fledged rocket, were the response to the Allied invasion of Europe. From June 1944 until February 1945, first the V1s and then the V2s hit England. The attacks differed significantly from the bombing raids earlier in the war. Although the damage was significant – whole streets could be devastated by a single weapon – the areas affected were geographically smaller and the attacks generally less concentrated than in the Blitz. Of course, Civil Defence services were better prepared, having learned from experience.

Just under 1½ million children and adults were evacuated from high-risk areas, of whom 275,000 were evacuated under the Government arrangements. This time their departure was delayed as troops were moved to the south coast for the Second Front.

Although essentially a Home Front service, the WVS found as early as 1940 that it was developing strong links with agencies and individuals overseas – not least because of the flood of clothing and other supplies sent from the USA and the Commonwealth. As a result, in 1940, the WVS Overseas Department was established. Throughout this early period, services similar to the British WVS also sprang up to meet the same sort of needs, and grew rapidly. The largest was in India, which had over 10,000 members, while the Nigerian WVS had over 3,000 members.

As the Allied forces pushed forward, the British WVS followed. The first British WVS to be sent overseas went to Italy and Algiers in 1944. Four WVS members followed the troops who landed on the Normandy beaches, providing the inevitable tea and sandwiches in Cherbourg but with the added benefits of a French chef, tinned food and a table-tennis table.

In 1945, WVS (SEAC), the WVS South East Asia Command, reported to the War Office in London, advising on providing mobile units to move up close behind the advancing army. The plan was to set up canteens and Welcome Clubs for troops as part of the Army Welfare authorities. Once again, the WVS filled the gaps and worked effectively across agency boundaries, filling in where the NAAFI could not. Requests for similar services came from around the world.

In Britain, just before the war ended, the Rehoming Department was established. Furniture was inevitably in short supply. Under this scheme, more than 9,000 tons of furniture, fixtures and fittings were donated mainly from rural areas, and redistributed to those whose homes had been destroyed or damaged in the raids. Shortages of food worsened. The service responded with a window-box and garden scheme, to grow flowers as well as fruit and vegetables in wrecked and rubble-strewn garden areas.

The official end of the war in Europe, VE Day on 8 May 1945, should have been the end of the WVS. By then, its British and overseas branches were involved in vital reconstruction work across the globe, later including Japan, near Hiroshima, where the Australian WVS took over when the British WVS left in 1949.

As the war ended and many WVS offices in Britain were claimed or reclaimed by local authorities, membership dropped. Many whose work had remained primarily in Civil Defence saw little future for the service and left. In wartime, although its original brief 'for Civil Defence' quickly disappeared in many areas, the WVS had become a vital part of many different services purely because of its ability to meet needs. Its good reputation with authorities and civilians was established. *Green Sleeves*, the WVS' official history, remarks that Lady Reading summed up the mood of its members: 'We know we look shabby and we know our members are not young but we are proud of the fact that we are trusted by ordinary people.'

In 1945, the new Labour Government announced that the service would drop the words 'for Civil Defence' from its title and continue 'possibly for two years'. The Government took over financial responsibility for many WVS offices from local councils, which improved the lot of remaining volunteers and staff immediately. But, as ever, it was practical necessity that drove home its value during peacetime. The floods of early 1947, coupled with worsening shortages meant that the WVS was as much in demand as it had been during the war. So it was no surprise, and a considerable relief, to the service and the general public when, in April of that year, the Home Secretary and his Scottish counterpart announced in the House of Commons that the WVS would be supported from central funds and 'fitted into the general pattern of Social Services tendered throughout the country'.

CHAPTER 4

Women's Land Army

The Women's Land Army drove tractors, ploughed fields, milked cows, made hay and played a full role in harvesting, threshing and thatching on farms across the country. It reclaimed land, herded sheep, cows and other livestock, and worked in orchards and market gardens. Rat-catching was a major, if unpopular, part of the work.

Wages were paid by farmers, in line with those agreed for women agricultural employees by the Agricultural Wages Board. This meant that a worker over the age of eighteen was to receive a minimum of £1 2s 6d (£1.12½p) a week (after deductions for board and lodging). Women in the WLA were more often known as 'Land Girls' and generally worked on the same terms and conditions as other agricultural employees. They had an agreed maximum working week (48 hours in the winter, 50 in the summer), guaranteed holidays and sick pay. Many worked a five-and-a-half-day week, taking Saturday afternoons and Sundays off. 'Some of the farmers did sometimes give a tip in appreciation. Either in cash or kind, usually eggs or other dairy produce – as we had a half day on a Saturday, I, like most of the girls, went home until Sunday evening. My Mum always appreciated these extras to supplement her rations – I wasn't able to give her any food coupons for such a short stay,' said Pat Vaughan (née Berry), although she also remembers being paid only 10s per week after deductions. In addition, each WLA volunteer stationed more than 20 miles from home could have a free rail warrant for a visit home every six months.

The Women's Land Army had its origins in the First World War: labour shortages following conscription of farm workers to the armed forces had caused concern as early as 1915, but it was another two years before the WLA was set up in 1917. At that point, it was discovered, according to Vita Sackville-West, that 'there was only about three weeks food supply in the whole country'. Quite what the Land Army could produce in that time is unclear but, nevertheless, the WLA was established, under the Ministry of Agriculture and the directorship of Dame Meriel Talbot. By 1918, 23,000 women had enrolled but it was disbanded the following year. The Scottish Land Army was organised under the direction of the Department of Agriculture for Scotland, in similar fashion to that of England and Wales.

During the 1930s, preparations for what seemed inevitable war included the WLA. This time, it was under the honorary directorship of Lady Denham, who made available her home, Balcombe Place, to act as its general headquarters. The WLA divided England and Wales into seven regions, each comprising one or

Who could resist such a welcoming invitation? (HMSO)

This leaflet set out the basic work of the WLA, what it meant to join and the pay and conditions.

more counties. Regional officers liaised with headquarters and inspected their regions regularly. Fifty-two county offices reported to those regions – larger counties such as Yorkshire had several such offices, whereas in other areas, small counties were often combined under a single office. Each county office had its own organising secretary, committee, sub-committees and local representatives. The local representatives, also known as village registrars, were, like the committee members, unpaid but everyone else in the offices had a salary. The county offices were the hub of the WLA organisation.

Most prospective Land Girls were interviewed at county level and by at least two people. A medical from an approved doctor followed and once an applicant had passed these hurdles, she was passed on to the county office. Training could be comprehensive or non-existent. Those who did receive instruction had practical and oral examinations in everything from milking and dairy work to pest destruction. WLA members had to be able to use all the usual farm equipment, and be capable of maintaining and cleaning it. A WLA correspondence course on agriculture covered topics such as the farm horse, including breeding and grooming, and arable crops and soil, with sections on types, temperatures and appropriate manuring. But equally, women might be directed on to the farms to start work immediately, learning as they went along.

Despite its military sounding title, the WLA was essentially civilian in structure. Volunteers were not, therefore, subject to military discipline and most were employed directly by the farmers for whom they worked. They could go to other jobs on other farms and farmers themselves could give their WLA women notice, along the same lines as other agricultural staff. As with many women's organisations of this time, the class element in the structure of the WLA brought its own flavour to the service: many local representatives were older, middle-class women who had lived in the district for some years. Their charges were often young girls who had come from the cities and industrial areas of the country with little or no understanding of the rural way of life. About a third of the recruits came from London and Middlesex, or from the industrial towns in the north of England. Many female conscientious objectors opted for work in the WLA.

The WLA local representative had the unenviable task of sorting out problems between farmers and their WLA workers. As part of this, she was expected to visit each volunteer in her district once a month, and prepare reports for the county offices. The form recorded whether billets were satisfactory, whether wages and overtime were correctly paid, how much time off was given each week and the arrangements for recreation. The section for general remarks notes that 'Comments on uniform should not be made on this form.'

The uniform was, by common consent, practical, quaint, comfortable – anything but fashionable. Given the number of women who opted for one service or another on the basis of the various uniforms on offer, this was no small matter. The basic WLA outfit consisted of brown brogues, brown corduroy or whipcord breeches, fawn knee-length woollen socks, a green V-necked pullover, fawn Aertex shirt and a brown felt cowboy-style hat. Added to this were a brown, military style short dress overcoat and Wellingtons or ankle boots. Special clothing included brown dungarees and the cow coat, a near knee-length garment in heavy brown cotton. The uniform was often ignored or frequently adapted; in summer weather, women would roll up their dungarees or cut them down to make shorts.

The tie was reserved for formal occasions, as was the armband. These were worn on the left arm, with red diamonds denoting length of service. The diamonds – half a diamond for each six months – were added as they were earned. The initial armband was green with red lettering, with a crown above the letters WLA. Very early versions followed the design of the First World War Land Army, of a red crown on a green background. After two years' service, the WLA volunteer replaced her initial armband with a similar green version, but with red piping and the two red diamonds already stitched on, one either side of

The Land Girl, *the official monthly publication of the Women's Land Army, was one attempt to combat homesickness among young and often isolated members.*

the crown. After four years, this was replaced with a band incorporating four full green diamonds on a red background. Those whose service lasted six years wore a yellow band with green features.

Initial reluctance among farmers to employ women to do men's jobs was rife and although Land Girls were clear that they were farm workers, not domestic staff, this was, unsurprisingly, often not appreciated. In the early years of the war, the call-up among agricultural workers was slow and the lack of farm work for the WLA meant that many women volunteered, trained and went home again. Those who were employed found that there was not always sufficient work on the farm to keep them busy.

Anne Hall, in her memoir, *Land Girl*, commented, 'I was told I was needed in the farmhouse to help Mrs Dale. When I protested that I was an outdoor worker, I was sent into the yard to chop wood and bring in coal. When, after lunch, we were asked to do the washing up and refused, and explained that Land Girls were not allowed to take on domestic work . . . this was not well received.' Anne and her WLA colleague Cara decided that the farm needed someone to help indoors and out, and that they should talk to their WLA representative, Mrs Payne. They told her how in winter the pressure would clearly be on them to work indoors. 'Mrs Payne said that the farm did not meet the regulations for employing WLA members. On September 14, we heard from Mrs Hope-Hannyngton in reply to our letter telling of our disatisfaction with conditions at the farm and she promised to come and see us the following week. However, our local rep visited

WLA proficiency tests covered just about every farm task imaginable, including milking and dairy work, tractor driving, outside garden and glasshouse work and pest destruction.

Standard Women's Land Army badge from the Second World War and after. The style of the crown is that of George VI.

and gave the Dales notice that we would be leaving in two weeks. That plan altered when the Dales asked us to leave on 21st September, as two former employees were returning to help on the farm and in the house.'

Some in the WLA were billeted in hostels, instead of farms, and some lived with other WLA members, while others found that they might be the only WLA worker attached to a farm. Homesickness was common and the sometimes isolated working conditions often added to the problem. A small gesture in that direction was the magazine the *Land Girl*, which was distributed nationally. The Land Army also had its own official song, 'Back to the Land'.

Iris Walters (née Daniels) joined in 1943.

The girls came from all walks of life and various parts of the country. We had some from Yorkshire and London. It must have been quite a culture shock for them. I, having been born in the country, didn't feel quite so bad.

I was employed by Hayward Bros. of 'Military Pickle' fame. They had two farms in Staplefield, Sussex, mostly arable, though we had a lot of sheep. We grew cauliflowers, onions, potatoes, as well as wheat.

Lady Dorothy Macmillan, wife of Sir Harold Macmillan, was our representative. She often had to put her boots on and walk across muddy fields to see us.

I was on the permanent staff but gangs of girls used to come to help with the hay making and hoeing; we really had lots of fun but it was very hard work and everyone was glad to get back to billets and fall into bed. After a while one got used to it!

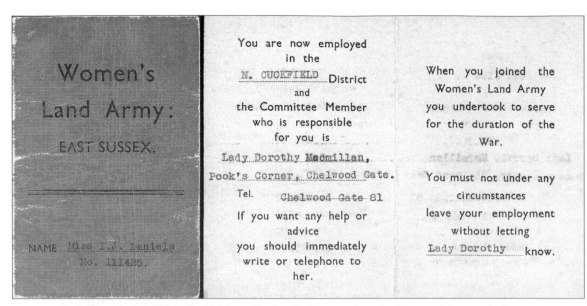

Lady Dorothy and Sir Harold Macmillan's telephone number, should you wish to use it, is on this WLA registration card.

Pat Vaughan had a varied career in the Women's Land Army:

[I wanted] to escape an airless environment indoors, on the switchboard at the civil defence headquarters in Wembley, north London.

By the winter of 1941, I yearned to be able to work in the fresh air and applied to join the Women's Land Army. My release from the Civil Defence was agreed and I joined the WLA early in 1942.

My initial training was at Cannington Farm Institute, near Bridgwater, in Somerset and for one month, I was trained in the skills required for general farming duties.

My first placement was at Corndean Hall, Winchcombe, on a dairy farm attached to the Manor House. I spent but a few weeks here, the only landgirl, working on milking and herd duties, before being sent to join another landgirl, on a chicken farm at Brent Pelham, near Buntingford, in Herts.

This was before the days of deep litter systems for keeping chickens, although they used a form of battery system for keeping their hens, but there was only one hen per cage. All egg collecting, feeding and cleaning was done by hand – usually by the men, employed full time.

As the hay making and harvest had to be brought in, we ladies of the WLA were asked to take over the chickens, whilst the men were employed outside for about two months. Not a pleasant job, especially in the summer heat, but it was here I met Lucy Whatmough and she and I became and remained very good friends.

When the hay and harvest was all in the barns, Lucy and I were sent to Pendley Manor, at Tring, in Hertfordshire. A hostel had been set up in the

Manor for about 30 Land Girls and from this base, gangs of us, sometimes a very small team, sometimes large gangs, were formed and sent out to farms in the Hertfordshire area, on a contract style of employment, to carry out any farming job required of us.

Land Girls were expected to turn their hands to all types of farm work in variable working conditions, as Pat quickly learned.

None of us knew what job was coming up, sometimes tractor work, for ploughing or field work such as potato or root crop planting or harvesting. (I cannot imagine what the reaction would be these days, but then, around October, many schools granted their pupils a very much longer half term, so they could also help with the potato harvest.)

Haymaking was always a popular task; fruit picking was, well, all right, but harvesting of grain crops, especially barley and white clover, was not only hard work but also a dusty filthy job (and not more than five inches of water in the bath afterwards, when you could get to one; no handy quick showers in those days).

Another sartorial deviation: Iris Daniels (left) and her friend Renée (right) are both wearing their dungarees with legs rolled up. Some just cut the dungarees off for the summer – tanned legs were one of the WLA's few aesthetic concessions. Renée has a bandage round her knee, protecting an injury caused when she was trying to duck a doodlebug (V1 flying bomb).

The most pleasant task was general farm work, when you could be milking, working with the cattle, sheep or other livestock.

Cleaning out the buildings after livestock had been housed in them for the winter was smelly, dirty work. It was a handfork and shovel job, the muck had to be loaded on to carts and then spread on the fields. Then return to cleanse and scrub the byres, whitewash the walls, disinfecting generally. The smell of Jeyes fluid still reminds me.

And then there was threshing. This was a winter job, usually between October and March. Outside work, in all weathers – the threshing equipment had to be pre-booked and so, whatever the weather, we had to carry on with the work.

What a noisy, heavy dirty job that was. Because I had less fear of height than most of the other girls, I usually got the job of taking the bags of chaff to the top of the barn, often via a ladder against the outside of the building.

Hazel Lillie of Brookers Farm ploughs a straight furrow in the tractor competition for Land Girls at Luddesdown Farm. Such competitions were a regular part of Land Army life – they were good for morale and demonstrated the high levels of skill WLA members achieved to sceptics. (Kent Messenger Group)

All this work on the farm, in all weathers, earned us the princely sum of ten shillings per week (50 pence) and out of this, we had to buy personal toiletries, make up, underclothes, off duty clothes – and to pay for any replacements of our 'best' uniform or working dungarees and jumpers.

Our working hours were very variable, probably between 40–48 hours in winter, but in summer when haymaking, you carried on until it was dusk – no extra pay for overtime. We were never expected to work on Sunday and it was most exceptional if we were not able to get away lunchtime on a Saturday.

In 1942, the WLA Timber Corps was established. Members, especially in Scotland, often lived in hutted camps. Annice Gibbs was in the Timber Corps:

I went to Chippenham in Wiltshire for training. We camped in Nissen huts – 12 women in each hut. The floors were rough concrete and in the centre was a

WLA uniform was not compulsory as this short skirt, worn in preference to dungarees, shorts or the instantly recognisable WLA knee breeches, shows.

slow combustion boiler which did not give out much heat. Each bed was made of slat wood called the Wooden McDonald and covered with only a thin biscuit palliasse for a mattress. It was cold and dreary. On our first day in the woods, wearing thick, heavy boots, gaiters and dungarees, we lifted the heavy pit-props on to a trailer. The women came from all walks of life and this heavy work was foreign to them. Needless to say the beds did not exactly soothe our aching bones.

We were quite a happy crowd really, but had our grumbles like everyone else. The food was the worst thing: the food itself was all right but the way it was cooked was a sacrilege. The rice was so hard it was like chicken feed, and the potatoes were cooked with the dirt still on them but we had to eat it or go without. We only had three sandwiches to last a full day in the woods, usually cheese. To make them go further and give extra warmth we turned them inside out and toasted them on our sandwich tins. They were always eaten by 10 in the morning because we were so ravenous, and by the afternoon we were physically exhausted through lack of food.

Minimal rations was not the only hardship Annice faced. She and her colleagues were expected to work in all conditions and their tasks were often physically demanding.

At first we were allowed to shelter from the rain but eventually we were issued with oilskins because of the time wasted in sheltering.

After our training, we soon got used to heavy work, such as lifting pit-props and cutting them into various lengths for the coalmines. Like everything else, there is a right way and a wrong way to lift up the pitprops and we learned how to keep the weight back away from our stomachs. Every prop was cut by hand, either with the cross-cut, or the bushman saw.

Wagon loads of pit-props would be driven through the woods by tractors and then they were transferred on to lorries. The need was so great they often did not have time to season properly and would split from the compression.

We worked with the New Zealanders, who were at the Saw Mills, and also the conscientious objectors.

There were masses of brushwood to be burned each day to keep the wood clear of debris. To keep the fires from spreading, each day before we left the operation, the fires were dug in. That meant digging a trench round the fire and making a barrier. Each night, the fires were inspected by the Forewoman, an important procedure as a spark could set a forest fire going.

The women then loaded the cut wood on to the trailers and drove them through the woods by tractor to the charcoal kilns. Here it was burned and the resulting charcoal used mainly for explosives, gasmask filters and smelting. In war time, it was one of our most essential products.

One of the worst jobs was stacking the sacks of charcoal on lorries to be dispatched to the station and then to be restacked again into the closed vans. The dust from the charcoal was choking and it penetrated right through our clothing to the skin making us so black we needed two baths to get clean.

However, there were some enjoyable aspects to working in the Timber Corps.

The very thin pine trees, about 2–3 inches in diameter, were measured into 20–25 feet lengths and used to enclose the POW camps. The larch trees were selected for telegraph poles and had to be about 72 feet long and absolutely dead straight.

Measuring was a job we liked because it gave a much needed break from heavy work. It entailed measuring trees, length by girth, and bringing it to cubic feet. These were the large trees for timber and the men were paid according to the cubic foot.

Sometimes we had to go to where the Italian POWs worked, to measure the trees. They were very well looked after and we were amazed to see them erecting field ovens. They cooked bacon and cabbage for their lunch and brewed delicious hot coffee.

Once, when it was raining, we were sat under a tree eating beetroot sandwiches. Needless to say, the rain soaked through to the beetroot, making the sandwiches soggy, red and none too appetising. We were fortunate, however, as they gave us some of their coffee and food. They were very surprised to see women felling trees.

Hostel life had its advantages and, for some, living in a stately home was one of them. This group picture, loaned by Joan Young (front row, fourth from left), was taken at Mentmore Towers.

By 1943, the initial problem of finding enough work for the Women's Land Army to do had long since faded away. The national diet became increasingly dependent on home-grown cereals and vegetables. By 1943, consumption of meat, fish, poultry, citrus fruits, oils and fats had reduced to the point where nearly half the average British diet consisted of home-grown grains and potatoes. Just about every available area of land had been converted into producing food and just about every conceivable job in agriculture was being done somewhere by a member of the Land Army, including rat-catching. Pat Vaughan continues:

It was the threshing that first made me really aware just what a problem the common rat was – corn ricks were a heavenly haven for these pests, where they had food in abundance, warmth and shelter.

I had been injured whilst out threshing and badly cut my thumb and was left behind at Pendley Manor for a day or two. I happened to read a notice on the board from the wartime Ministry of Agriculture and Fisheries (who were our 'Lords and Masters'). It appeared they had decided the rat problem was not getting any better and so called for 'Volunteers' to go on a course to learn about pest control.

I volunteered – the only one from Pendley Manor. I was sent to St Albans, for a two week course so that we could learn all about the handling, mixing and use of rat poisons.

We had to sit for an examination at the end – I was pleased to learn I had obtained a very high pass mark.

On my return to Pendley Manor, I was teamed up with Fred, who was assisted by a young lad. The three of us then became the official Rat Catchers for North West Hertfordshire. No increase in my weekly wage was forthcoming.

Pat describes exactly what her new job entailed.

Our usual method of working was for Fred to drop me off at the first farm with all my equipment, a dessert spoon, attached to a 3-foot cane and a draw string bag, made of American Cloth (cotton material, coated on one side with a water proof surfacing) to keep my bait dry, whilst he, with his lad, carried on to the next job.

I didn't take the poisons with me every day – you worked on a 1:3:5 basis. First day you looked for rat trails and holes, making, if necessary, safe areas where bait and poison could be placed. You then baited as required. This bait was usually oats, wheat or sometimes sausage rusks and you used your own judgment as to the best to use, having decided what food was normally available to the rats in that locality.

On the third day, you returned to check what bait had been taken, replenishing where necessary and on the 5th day, you mixed your poison with whatever bait you had used, adding this mixture to the baited area. Making as sure as you possibly could, that only rats could get to the poisoned bait.

We then usually returned after a few days to try and find out just how successful we had been. One day, I was working near a river bank in an area quite badly infested. I don't like thunderstorms and one day a very severe one started. Rather than trying to take cover under some trees on my own, I sat in the open, amongst the rats, just so that I had company of some sort during the storm.

When I returned to the hostel at the end of the day and related what I had done to the other girls, the Hostel Supervisor realised I was working on my own for most of the time. It was then it was decided I should have another land girl (untrained), to work with me, in the same manner that Fred had the lad.

Although Pat no longer worked alone, she and her assistant still had difficulty reaching their sites, and the work was often unpleasant.

No extra Jeep was provided and so my little team used public transport or whatever transport we could scrounge when Fred and myself were going out in opposite directions.

If we were called in because a gang out on threshing were getting towards the bottom of a rick, we went as a combined team, including Fred's terrier dogs. After setting up a small meshed wire netting fence around the rick and threshing machinery, we, the four of us, the farmer's and Fred's dogs and sometimes the farmer worked inside this area.

We had armed ourselves with sticks, spades or whatever we regarded as being suitable, trouser bottoms tied up with string around the ankles (so that no rat could run up inside the trouser leg) and as they ran from the bottom of the rick, you killed as many as you possibly could.

It was a very noisy affair, the traction engine was driving the threshing machine via a long endless belt (totally unguarded) and the mechanical noise from the machinery, the dogs barking excitably and occasional screams from one or other of the Land Girls working on the threshing, as rats ran over their feet – especially as they neared the bottom of the rick.

When all the grain had been threshed out, the base was then cleared away, to make sure no rats were left. The terriers were incredibly efficient – they just grabbed a rat, a quick shake of their head to kill it and on to the next one. Some rats escaped over the wire netting, but a dog followed and surprisingly few got clean away.

How many rats got killed in this fashion? A lot depended on how the rick had been built in the first place but in a rick built of branches and brushwood, I remember a total, killed in one day, of around 360. The figure stuck in my mind as I can recall the farmer saying 'One for each day of the year then.'

Another location usually infested with rats was the central collecting points for Pig Swill – in wartime Britain, food waste (potato peel, pea, bean and brassica waste and food left over at meals) was not thrown away, but put into the street 'Pig Bin' which was collected by the local authority and taken to a depot to be boiled and used as pig food.

Another pest we were called upon to deal with, was the rabbit: funnily enough, when called to deal with them, we were never able to get to the farm before Friday. We used ferrets – Fred's, of course – and purse nets and after the girls and the lad had enough freshly killed rabbit to take home after work on Saturday, Fred was able to find a 'home' for the rest, I think with the local butcher.

Towards the end of the war, Pat decided on a change of scene.

In 1944, I was transferred to Harrow Borough Council as their official rat-catcher. A vacancy had been advertised and I had applied: it was much nearer home and considerably more money. I was also able to get a full allocation of clothing coupons.

This was an entirely different sort of job – it was an urban area and the rats were in sewers, under sheds, buildings and paving stones, in cellars and even in roofs. The Pig Clubs were also here and the back of a works unit or an allotment was the much more usual site used.

I still had to use my long handled spoon and my bait bag though – it was about this time that Warfarin started to become available and was much safer to handle than my previous poisons, although still very dangerous.

Now in urban Harrow, I was increasingly called upon to deal with and remove wasp nests.

In the summer of 1944 I got married and the Methodist Minister, so amused by the work I did, insisted on recording my occupation on my marriage certificate.

Post-war Britian faced food shortages which actually increased as it struggled to pay off its war debts and rebuild a peacetime economy. In the period immediately after the war, food rationing in particular increased and as a result, the Land Army carried on until 1950, when it was disbanded. It had provided over 90,000 women and girls to work on the land during the Second World War – four times more than the 23,000 who had made up the WLA during the First World War.

CHAPTER 5
Civilian Work

Working women were among the first casualties of the Second World War. Only 9 hours after war was declared, the liner *Athenia* was torpedoed in the Atlantic by a U-boat. On board were 1,418 passengers. The five stewardesses on board helped save American and Canadian passengers trapped in the dining room. Four of them, Alison Harrower, Margaret Johnston, Jessie Lawler – all British – and a Canadian, Hannah Baird, gave their lives in the rescue and are commemorated today in Merchant Navy memorials at Tower Hill and Halifax, Nova Scotia. Merchant Navy women continued to play their part throughout the war. In 1941, the MN's only female qualified ship's engineer, Victoria Drummond, brought her ship through a heavy bombing raid and was awarded the MBE.

Women were already beginning to enter the workforce in greater numbers before the war. But what might have been gradual and quiet progress into many previously all-male preserves was thrown centre stage with the direction of female labour into key areas. In wartime, much was made of women's inferior physical strength, as if this were an inevitability on an individual basis, rather than a product of comparing broad averages. The WLA produced a chart assessing the relative productivity of men and women in various agricultural jobs which purported to show that only in fruit picking were women more productive. In practice, the issue of productivity was more complex. In some areas, notably light engineering, women tended to have more nimble fingers, making them better than men at some of the work.

One major difference between men and women in the workplace was absenteeism. Ministry of Labour figures put absenteeism for men at 6 to 8 per cent and 12 to 15 per cent for women. In its 1943 publication *War Factory*, Mass Observation commented that at the factory under its scrutiny:

> . . . absenteeism is not bad: it is barely ten per cent (for all reasons), considerably lower than most factories in the district. Such as there is, other than for illness, is mainly of a pretty aimless kind; going to dances and then waking up too late in the morning to catch the 'bus and so on. . . . But on the whole far more time is probably wasted by dawdling inside the factory than ever by taking days off.
>
> As in the case of other kinds of slacking, there is no pressure of public opinion against it. Girls will come in on Monday and describe to the whole bench just how they managed to get off on Saturday and just what lies they are

One of the best-known posters of the war, drawn by Donald Zec. (HMSO)

proposing to tell to the foreman, and receive nothing but sympathy and interest from their hearers, mixed with a certain amount of envy.

Mass Observation reported that many women at that factory did their knitting during working hours, concealing the pins and yarn under the bench. It also observed that many of the female employees disliked working under female charge hands as they were stricter than their male counterparts, and that women would take time off to go shopping – definitely a 'woman's job' at that time.

Engineering had been an increasingly popular careeer choice for women in the 1930s. Wartime needs accelerated their introduction into some areas. Vera Costan was a court dressmaker in Liberty's in London when the outbreak of the Second World War was declared. Almost immediately, she said,

We all got our cards.

I saw an advert for Post Office Engineers, wanted at Elmbridge Exchange at Surbiton in Surrey. I lived in Wimbledon and it would be easy to get a train and quiet (so I thought), so I applied and was taken on. We had six weeks initial training in Belmont. We learned the names of all the tools, the different kinds of wires, the connections with the exchange and how the exhange itself worked – all very different from today.

Women were generally able to work more quickly and accurately on some of the engineering tasks that required nimble fingers. (Kent Messenger Group)

Next we went to Elmbridge. There were ten of us at first although that number dwindled. We met the men working there and were shown around the exchange. The man in charge of us was a Mr Williams and none of them envied him his job! 'Willie and his Girls' they would say. He had a small room upstairs and it was there we had to meet each morning. We worked 8.30 to 5.30pm, and Saturday, 8.30 to 1pm. On our first day, we all went to the store room and were given a real leather Gladstone bag to carry our tools. It was as much as we could do to lift it. Later it was replaced by a satchel. There were so many screwdrivers, hammers, bradawls and so on –

each one had to be signed for and if we lost any, we had to replace them ourselves. Once, working at a factory, I left my bag overnight and next day, the whole lot had been stolen.

In the early days things did not always go according to plan.

We did nothing unless it was on the 'Advice Note'. We were each given two or three advice notes to get on with, in case someone was out. We used buses all the time. My first job was at Richmond in Surrey. I was so nervous but it was an ordinary direct line. The lady in the flat was expecting a baby. Her husband was overseas and she was glad for someone to

A woman draining a locomotive. A national agreement worked out with the rail unions meant that after a specified period a woman railworker in wartime was paid the standard rate of the man she replaced. (Kent Messenger Group)

talk to. I wired the 'phone, checked the outside wiring – always overhead or underground then – and thought I had done a pretty good job. But when I tested it, nothing. I checked all my notes and everything else. I was there until five o'clock. I reported to the exchange, the next morning and told the men it didn't work. They said I had not had the line connected at the exchange. Lesson One.

As we got more experience and confidence, we went to the big factories all on munitions night work and so on. They were always needing more extensions or new lines.

Later, I went on another course and learned to fit small switchboards. We sometimes had to call on the men for advice but we hated doing that and they weren't very forthcoming – they didn't like us doing the same job as them.

Oh, but how they went about their working day! They had vans and could go home for lunch or sit in the vans for an hour. We had to find a café and would be lucky to get a sandwich.

There were unpleasant sides to the job too:

One of the most distressing things was when, after an air raid, we had to go through the wreckage and recover any telephones, cable, fittings and anything else we could salvage as no new telephones were being made in those days. There were heaps of them at the exchange. Now and again we had to stay in for a week, go through it all and pick out the best bits to make new 'phones.

Then one of the men would give it the once over and it was put in store. We were often short of 'phones. When people had been evacuated, we had to get the keys and take all the telephones out and disconnect at the exchange. When people started to return, when it was quiet, we had to get the advice note to put it all back. Mr Williams sometimes would turn up to keep tabs on us. One time, we were at a very big house in Sheen. The garden was very overgrown and neglected. Two of us were rewiring inside and out, plugging the walls and so on. I was measuring up the outside cable. I stepped back to survey and went flat on my back into what was supposed to be a 'lily pond'. It was thick mud and smelly. Kath, my mate, said, 'Go up to one of the rooms, take all your clothes off. I'll lay them out to dry in the sun while I finish the outside.' So I sat on the floorboards in this room upstairs. Suddenly Mr Williams

Anything that made a female factory worker's life easier had to be good for other women too.

appeared and asked Kath, 'Where's Vera?' Kath said, 'She's upstairs and she has no clothes on.' Well, Mr Williams must have thought she was joking and I was skiving – he came upstairs to find me! Later, I had to dress to go home on the 'bus and I smelt terrible. By now we had these thick serge trousers which were awful anyway in summer.

I don't remember ever having any identification and people often refused to believe we were the engineers so we would have to make another appointment for another day.

I learned a lot in those years. At least I was able to put shelves up and knock nails in and I have still got some of my tools in case I want to do it now.

Before the war, even factories employing both men and women often segregated their workers according to the different jobs each would do. In wartime, an initial and frequent problem was the need to provide separate toilets and washrooms for men and women, now working together in most areas of a factory.

Eddie Gardner worked for Venner Time Switches from 1936 (when he was fourteen) to 1947.

The company was at Shannon Corner, New Malden in Surrey, and made time switches for lamp posts, telephone kiosks, shop windows and so on.

Before the war, the machine shop was entirely staffed by men, mostly fairly young. Women worked in a separate part of the factory, the assembly hall, where they carried out various duties such as laquering the brass plates visible on the time switch.

It was a fairly harsh regime but it changed as soon as the women started to arrive at the machine tool shop. By 1938, a few women had started in the machine shop. But by 1940, I would guess that about 75 per cent of the staff were women.

Up until 1939, there was no official tea break. In the morning and afternoon, tea was brought round by a tea boy and he could also get rolls, sandwiches, cakes, cigarettes and sweets. But when women were brought into the workforce, a regular tea break was arranged for 10–15 minutes each morning and afternoon. Before, tea and food was taken at your machine and you did not stop work. Now the break was taken in the canteen.

As the canteen did not provide hot meals, a new staff restaurant was built by about 1941 and this did provide hot meals and it had a stage. The BBC programme Worker's Playtime was broadcast from Venner's on one occasion.

Factory catering often highlighted differences: it was reported that women generally opted for salads and lighter meals, while men preferred something more substantial and stodgy puddings. Eddie Gardner continues:

I worked in the gear-cutting section where, before the war, there were about 18 hobbing machines and three larger machines. It was normal for a young man to operate two or three machines but when women took over, they worked only one machine each and had stools to sit on.

In late 1939, another eight machines were installed. Of course, one person per machine increased production. Then part-timers came in and it was found that two part-timers could produce more than one full timer.

My friend and I became Setter Operators and set up the machines. Various gears and other tools had to be changed depending on the type of gear to be cut and how many teeth were to be cut but I can only remember one woman becoming a setter operator.

The women usually wore a scarf or tied their hair back but there were a few accidents of this type with them getting their hair caught up in the machinery.

Before the war, smoking was allowed only for half an hour in the morning and in the afternoon but that changed too and soon smoking was allowed any time of the day or night.

By 1938, when I was promoted to the Hobbing Section, it was the practice to give each machine operator a bonus once a week. The under foreman would come round with book in hand and a great deal of silver in his pocket and place anything from one to three shillings on the workbench for you to pick up but of course if you had displeased your chargehand in any way, you may pick up nothing. In 1939, the job of paying out the bonus was given to a young lady but by 1940, piecework was introduced to increase production, so the old bonus system ended.

Younger people were often sent to do heavy work. Doreen Perkins went to a brickworks.

I worked in the press sheds. I went in when I was 17. I thought it would be better than going away from home. I earned 2 pounds a week. We had to take the bricks and load them on to the bogeys (four wheeled trucks). It was very cold, especially in the winter because the press sheds were all open. I worked with 2 colleagues. I wore a bib and brace outfit in the summer, and a boiler suit and a coat in the winter.

The hours were very long: Mondays 6am to 6pm; some days we worked until 6.30, some days until 7.30. There was no proper canteen so we used to make toast on the stove. I only weighed 7 stone 12 pounds but I didn't feel exhausted. We were all boys and girls of the same ages working together as a group. There were about 10 or 12 of us altogether and we enjoyed ourselves.

We had three presses between 2 girls. We could not let the presses stand idle at all. You had to be really quick as they were coming down all the time. It was hard work but it was surprising how you did pick yourself up when you finished work.

They closed the brickworks after 2 or 3 years and some of the women went to work in other brickyards in the area. But I didn't – I went instead to work in a shop selling baby clothes and leather goods.

Transport, especially on the railways or the buses, was an area where pay and conditions were generally better than average and, as in the First World War, 'clippies' were often in the thick of the danger. 'Clippies' were women who clipped the tickets on buses and trams to mark where the passengers boarded. Elizabeth Jackson was first a conductor and then a driver on trams in Liverpool from 1940 to 1946.

We were supposed to stop and find shelter wherever we could during raids. One Saturday evening, about 6pm, the air raid wardens stopped the tram and told passengers and crew to take shelter in the basement of the New Theatre (which used to be called the Prince of Wales Theatre). We were there all night, until the early hours. During a lull in the bombing, the driver and I asked if we could go and find something to eat. Across the road in Church Street, there was a Forces Canteen. At first, we were refused entry, because it was only for people in uniform. 'But we are in uniform' I said, showing them my brand new City of Liverpool Corporation Tram uniform and my trainee conductor's badge. When we had finished a huge meal of sausage, egg and chips, we went back to the shelter to tell our colleagues. But we were all back within five minutes – an incendiary had hit the canteen and it was in flames.

I had another narrow escape, in May 1941 when I was going down Mount Pleasant. The driver was forced to stop as things were getting a bit scary: we could hear the bombs and see the fires on the skyline. The tram was full of soldiers carrying all their kit — they were going to Lime Street station, returning from their leave. I persuaded the driver to divert up Clayton Square so he could drop the soldiers off at the station.

On the return journey, the driver and I were stopped by a policeman at the Adelphi. He said we could go no further as the road had been bombed.

We spent the night in a shelter and made our way back to the tram the following day. As we went, we saw an enormous bomb crater in the road, where normally we would have stopped had we kept to our normal route.

That weekend, I went on duty at 11am on the Saturday and didn't get back to the depot until Sunday afternoon. During that time no one knew where we were as all telephone lines were down and, with bomb craters on the roads, we just couldn't get in touch with the depot, some 7 miles out of town.

My parents afterwards always said that they had 3 sons fighting in the Army overseas, a daughter somewhere in England with the ATS and I was the only one living at home – and the only one reported missing.

John Kirk was evacuated with his mother, father and sister to Burton on Trent.

My Dad was a baker and that was a reserved occupation and he got a job there.

My mother became a signal lady on the railways. Her railway uniform was culottes and a jacket – all in navy blue. It was a case of going on to the railway or going into a munitions factory.

My mum was trained in the box by the person who already worked there. There were 2 8-hour shifts a day – 6am to 2pm, then 2pm to 10pm. Her signals were on the brewery line which went down to the main line. There were 3 or 4 level crossings on the line too. She controlled one box and one level crossing. The level crossing had to be opened and closed by hand.

You had to turn the wheel to open the crossing gates then send a morse code signal to notify them the gates were open or closed. You would send one 'ding' and they would answer with 2 'dings' and you would send a 'ding' back. There would be about 2 trains an hour.

I used to go and see my mother in the signal box. My sister worked in the brewery offices. It was very formal – Miss Kirk, Miss This and Miss That. I was too young to do anything but I used to go and see her after school.

Every week, she would go up to the railway station to get her pay. She would give her number in at the office and they would tell you how much you had earned.

War regulations meant paperwork in abundance – there were forms for every imaginable task in every imaginable area, and administrative posts to go with them. 'Ninkey' Coe describes her experiences.

I got a job at the County Offices clerking for the War Agricultural Commission, which issued feeding stuff coupons for farm animals. This was a complete shambles to start with; the system was ludicrous, and must have been done by someone who had absolutely no knowledge of farming.

The system this genius had worked out was that if your farm had 200 acres and 100 cattle that should supply enough grass to feed them. Of course, not all farms have arable land, and also cattle need more than grass.

We had one desperate farmer who threatened to shoot himself in the office as he said his pedigree herd was

A woman connecting a hose between railway rolling stock. Thousands of women worked on just about every task involved in keeping the railways running. By 1943, more than 105,000 railwaywomen had replaced 103,000 railwaymen, who had been released to join the armed forces. Before the war, just 26,000 women had worked for the industry, mainly in clerical jobs. That situation returned after the war. (Kent Messenger Group)

clammed to death [starving]. The boss was out, and we had thousands of coupons which we could give out. I grabbed a little bundle and gave them to him, and when the boss returned he agreed.

So we used our own judgement, and six months later we had a memo from the Ministry saying 'use your own discretion with distribution'. If we had waited, half the livestock in Derbyshire would have starved to death.

Demand from the forces for nurses inevitably rises during wartime. In the Second World War, the anticipated shortage of civilian nurses that this would cause was made more serious by the increased demand on a Home Front suffering large numbers of civilian casualties as a result of aerial bombardment. Trained nurses were needed to take charge of first-aid posts under the ARP scheme. Nurses from many organisations, including the British Red Cross Society, Order of St John of Jerusalem, the First Aid Nursing Yeomanry and the Voluntary Aid Detachments, were called on to help at home and overseas.

Nurses who had retired or stopped work on marriage were recalled to fill the breach. The Emergency Medical Service of the Ministry of Health had, by the end of September 1939, enrolled 15,000 trained nurses and 20,000 trained auxiliaries. A further 76,000 had been accepted for training as auxiliaries.

One of the smallest nursing groups was the River Ambulance Service. At the outbreak of the war, this consisted of three trained nurses and ten auxiliaries working 24-hour shifts on Thames steamers which had been fitted out as hospital ships.

By contrast, VADs (members of the Voluntary Aid Detachment) were found in just about every wartime setting imaginable. Formed in 1910, the VAD was created especially to provide nurses to meet anticipated wartime shortages. More than 48,000 VADs in 1,800 detachments were serving at the outbreak of the First World War. About 126,000 VADs served during the course of the conflict, of whom 129 were killed. VADs worked on the Home Front and overseas, and their wide-ranging duties included taking care of injured military personnel and civilians in transit, clerking, ambulance driving, cooking and running dressing stations and emergency hospitals. Before the Second World War, VADs were reorganised so that they could supplement general medical services when mobilisation for war began. Now, VADs had to be able to move around. Those who could not, were asked to transfer to the Nursing Auxiliary. In the Second World War, VADs enlisted in Britain totalled 15,000 and were drawn from the Red Cross and the Order of St John and St Andrew's Ambulance Association. They were civilians and so not counted as part of the auxiliary forces.

Mary Buck (née Blackburn) was twenty-eight years old when war was declared in 1939.

I was immediately 'called up' to a military hospital in Yorkshire.

After a year I answered an advertisement in *The Times* for VAD personnel to staff a Red Cross Hospital for Officers' wives, in Fulmer, Buckinghamshire, run by VADs and trained staff, instigated by Lady (then Mrs) Churchill. The VADs made themselves useful in various ways, in the nursery with new babies, fetching and carrying trays, bedpans, etc., cooking for patients and staff on rations. Lady Churchill and the Duchess of Gloucester, as members of the Committee, came regularly to see if any equipment was wanted. In the kitchen, under a Cordon Bleu Cook (from the Red Cross), we competed to see who could make the lightest scones for them.

On one occasion, Lady Churchill offered to give the Head Cook and I a lift to London in her bullet-proof car, with flags flying on the radiator, where we were dropped at a London hospital to visit one of the VADs who had had an operation. She rang for someone to provide us with a cup of tea, which prompted the reply that they didn't serve tea to visitors – so we drank some of my friend's tea in tooth mugs.

Nurses at work in the kitchen of Fulmer Chase, a hospital for officers' wives in Buckinghamshire. Mary Buck is third from left (and inset).

As Fulmer was rather isolated we had visitors to entertain the pregnant ladies. Among them was Constance Spry who showed slides of her flower and vegetable arrangements. Having no flowers in her bedroom that night, I managed to produce a half dead dahlia floating in an ash-tray.

It was of course vital that student nurses continued to train during the war and by the end of the conflict, training for State Registered Nurses had been reduced from four to three years. Moira Macleod joined the British Red Cross in 1940.

I was under 18, so was not allowed to do full-time nursing. I stayed in Bayswater with my parents, spending two days a week at Paddington General Hospital when the Blitz started in London in August 1940.

I was also sent to a school taken over as an emergency centre for people made homeless.

This entailed walking through the streets in the blackout through the bombing and hoping not to be hit by bits of falling metal – usually the shell casing from anti-aircraft guns. As I was only part-time, I was not issued with a tin hat. I did two whole nights a week at the Emergency Shelter. There were two of us Red Cross nurses. Our function was to give reassurance (though actually it was the other way around!) and prepare the babies' feeds.

Our outdoor uniform was a long navy raincoat with brass shoulder plates denoting your detachment: London Chelsea 98, in my case, and a small navy cap with a Red Cross badge.

Later, Moira Macleod and a friend went to the North Middlesex Hospital in London to train as State Registered Nurses.

The hospital was large, about 1,200 beds. Much of the building was old. However the nurses' home was modern and comfortable.

In early 1944, the hospital was hit by a number of bombs dropped by a single aircraft. Several people were killed including three members of staff.

I was on night duty as a theatre nurse and was on my meal break at the time. I heard the plane dive and threw myself and a junior nurse on to the floor; there was an almighty bang and I found myself shouting 'We're all right. We're all right.'

All the lights were out but the ward was on fire, which gave some illumination. The lifts were out of action. I ran outside, trying to get back to the theatre, and tripped and fell heavily because of debris on the path. I went back to the main building and saw a former male patient, wandering around in a daze. He had come from the top floor ward and together we went up the stairs, scrambling over debris to find a part of the top ward sheered off, the roof gone and all the windows blown out. The one night nurse (the other was on her break) put her tin hat on her head and we helped her carry patients down the stairs, lay them on the floor and go back up for more. By this time, fireman and rescue teams were milling around.

After a while I returned to the operating theatre and found all quiet there, with the emergency lighting in operation.

There were more than the usual number of staff around as other nurses came in to help. A doctor was having bits of shrapnel picked out of his back. My friend flung her arms around me and said, 'Mac, I thought you'd been killed.' I then realised the sight I presented: black with debris and dust, my cap blown away, bleeding from superficial scratches. I was given an anti-tetanus shot and cleaned up a bit. Then another fellow student nurse, well-liked and respected, was brought in badly injured. Our staff stood ready as she was briefly examined to see if she needed surgery, but before she could be helped, she died. That was a terrible moment; we clung to each other and wept.

After a long night, I went back to my room on the night nurses' corridor. I found the whole wing had been bombed.

Moira experienced other distressing situations on a daily basis.

Penicillin was available but its use was strictly controlled, for use on Service personnel and air raid casualties only. We found this very frustrating when someone was ill with a condition which responded to penicillin. There were many infections and illnesses and on the surgical wards, where wounds had to be dressed. There were no disposable articles then. Gas gangrene would sometimes occur and infections such as meningococcal meningitis. Sometimes fatal, tuberculosis was very common and some student nurses had contracted the illness or were found to have a shadow on their lungs when X-rayed for their first medical examination.

The death rate was so high by modern standards but few patients died without a nurse to hold their hand, if no relatives were with them. Most poignant were children. Many suffered from pneumonia as a result of . . . [living in] . . . cold houses with windows blown out or drafty air raid shelters and coming into contact with a wide mix of people, and infections.

Rules were strict: unless the child was on the dangerously ill list, parents' visits were restricted and little toddlers would cry in vain for their mothers. Some children were put on general wards, their cots placed between men and women who would try to comfort them when the air raids were on.

Despite the demands of the job and the 'miniscule pay of a student nurse', Moira remembers the nurses were able to enjoy a good social life. A turn of duty that finished at 6 p.m. was especially popular, as it allowed them to get to the centre of London for the evening's entertainments. In September 1945, Moira Macleod passed her SRN examinations having spent three years and nine months at the North Middlesex Hospital.

Just as it would be near impossible to list comprehensively the range of organisations of nursing services, so too would it be impossible to detail fully the range of civilian work women carried out in this and other areas during wartime. Traditionally, female professions were inevitably changed by the wartime experience but it was some years before married women were allowed to work as nurses. Given its origins in the Crimean War and its military style structure, it is perhaps not surprising that nursing felt less need than other professions to adapt, being well organised to cope with the demands of both peacetime and wartime working.

Elsewhere, women working in what had been male areas were always viewed as temporary help, required only in wartime. This was often reflected in their relatively low status within the workplace. But an influx of even temporary workers who remained part of the working environment for years inevitably had an impact on many industries' attitudes to the way they treated their permanent, peacetime and predominantly male staff. Wartime conditions meant that staff canteens became widespread and were refined in many factories after the war. Other industries, notably the furniture trade, found some women could do as good a job as some men and could be paid less too.

As for the women themselves, even if they returned willingly to the home, they found their experiences had broadened their outlook. Differential rates of pay for men and women persisted until the Equal Pay Act of 1970 was fully implemented in 1975. It was only the Sex Discrimination Act of 1975 that ended the widespread practice among employers of specifying in advertisements whether a man or woman would be taken on to fill a vacancy. But by that time, public opinion was ahead of the game: thirty years earlier, too many women had done the same job as men for sex discrimination on pay and access to jobs to seem anything other than arbitrary.

CHAPTER 6

War Weapons

The Ministry of Aircraft Production was established in May 1940, mainly so Churchill could give his friend Lord Beaverbrook, who had made the *Daily Express* the best-selling newspaper of the time, direct control over production. Britain's rearmaments programme was accelerated and aircraft production was of particular concern. Factories began working 24 hours a day, seven days a week and many worked 12-hour shifts. Pay was good for many in this type of work – better than the national average. The workforce in a typical factory comprised women and men, either reserved because of their specific skills or unfit for active service.

The German army swept through Belgium and Holland, and the fear of invasion became real. Holidays were cancelled. Workers regularly slept at their factories, either because the late finish to one shift meant there was little point in going home, or because air raids made travel impossible. Eventually, Ernest Bevin stepped in and made a maximum 60-hour week compulsory for women. He extended it the next month to men and advised on the importance of rest days. Lord Beaverbrook took little notice and the seven-day working week continued. Aircraft production soared, as energy and resources were diverted from production of other, equally essential, supplies such as tanks.

Midlands-based private engineering and aircraft firms like Rolls Royce and Armstrong Siddeley were fully engaged in war production and raids on Coventry and Derby were aimed at disrupting their output. Gladys Reeves recalls her work at the Armstrong Siddeley plant.

I had been married for just 10 months when the Second World War reached its climax. I was living in Rugby at the time. Having no children, I had either to take people into my home, have a baby or go out to work. I chose the latter.

My husband was already working at the Armstrong Siddeley factory at Coventry. He was a toolmaker and cutter/grinder so he was vital to the war effort.

So he got me a job in the machine shop. If my husband was going to lose his life, I felt that I would prefer it to happen to me too so that we would remain together even in death. Working in the same place made this a realistic possibility. It sounds morbid but that is how we felt at the time.

We were both on nights so we had to leave our home at six o'clock. The train left the station for Coventry at 6.30. Sometimes the German planes made a

Merely to remind you that . . . .

TIME FLIES

(and especially where urgent repair jobs are concerned)

Another Works Urgency appeal

One of a pair of cartoons drawn by the artist Fougasse, which marked various initiatives to keep up production in the factories.

nuisance of themselves trying to bomb or machine gun it. When this happened, we hid down the railway embankment. It was exhausting – we still had to do a night's work from 8pm to 7.30.

The journey to work might be hazardous, but conditions inside the factory were no better.

Often when we did get to work, the air raid siren would go so we had to shut the machinery down and go to the air raid shelter. To me this always seemed funny because it had been built inside the factory. If the factory was bombed, the air raid shelter would have gone too.

We expected bombers to come every night, but soon got used to it. When the attack was not too bad, we just donned our tin hats and hoped for the best. But as time passed, the raids became heavier. They even started shooting down the barrage balloons so they could get through to us. After one night shift, we walked along Park Road, to see the devastation the bombers had caused. The houses were all gone. Fires were still burning. People were still looking for their loved ones and salvaging what they could from the rubble. Tired firemen were packing up hoses and smelling of blood, smoke and sweat.

The push was on to make as many aircraft as possible so this work was labour intensive: eight people are visible working on this single fuselage. (Jonathan Falconer Collection)

I saw a small boy of about four years old with no cheeks to his bottom. He was crying for his mummy and I carried him as gently as I could to an ARP worker, trying not to cause him any more pain.

We were very tired after a night's work and on the train we always sang songs and told jokes to keep awake. If we hadn't we could have travelled on to London!

One night, we lost the factory roof when a bomb hit the graveyard next to us. The next thing we knew, bodies, skeletons and coffins were flying everywhere and through the roof like a scene from a horror film.

Soon afterwards, I left Coventry as I became pregnant.

When I had my baby, my husband had a night off work to be with me. He was called before a tribunal at work. He was found guilty and fined heavily because there had been no one to replace him. But he did not care as long as the baby and I were all right. It was worth every penny!

Margaret Stevenson (née Westley) was one of thousands of women who went to work in the 1930s when their husbands became unemployed in the depression.

I started working in 1937 in a furniture factory but when the war started, it was turned over to munitions.

I worked on the conveyer belts and as the ammunition boxes got to me they already had the bottoms in and the holes drilled and I had to drill the fixings into the holes, putting in the two and a half inch screws. I used to have to use a big electric screwdriver – it was terribly hard work. I didn't think I'd stick it at first.

The wages there were 1/- an hour and then after three months it would go up to 1/3d. Men were paid more – they got 1/8d an hour to start with.

We had Woolwich Arsenal inspectors who passed them out. My number was 177 and that went on all the boxes I worked on.

The factory had men and women. The men were mainly those unfit for active service.

We worked a 45-hour week. You could also go in Saturday mornings. You did 8am to 5pm with a quarter of an hour break and a lunch break.

Smoking was not allowed. You could buy snacks to eat and we had a chap who was good on the piano so we used to sing a lot of the time. The social life there carried on through the war. We would have factory dances with a band once a year.

Ag, my sister in law, and her husband Art, lived with us so Ag looked after my daughter, Sylvie. I didn't worry about her usually because I knew she was in good hands with Ag but one day at work they sent for me because a bomb had fallen near the school. I left in such a flurry but she was all right.

My husband worked in Leavis', the sawmills, cutting up the timber as it came off the barges and he got 1/11d an hour. So I said, find me some work over there. That way we could work in the same place and I would be earning more than I was on the boxes. One day he said I could start there on a particular day but it was Sylvie's birthday so I said I wouldn't go.

Anyway, I went over there eventually and stayed until the end of the war. I really enjoyed it.

Doreen Perkins found there were advantages to working in a parachute factory. 'The hours were 7.30am to 5.30pm. It was all women. The machinists worked in groups and so did we. The parachutes were laid out on benches for folding. You had to fold the finished 'chute in the right way. You could keep the silk off-cuts to make petticoats and other underwear – you had to get the stuff where you could.'

By common consent, one of the most dangerous areas of work into which women were directed was munitions. The factories were massive. ROF Swynnerton, a filling factory near a small village of that name in Staffordshire, had more than 2,000 small buildings employing between 20,000 and 30,000 workers. Like many such factories, it was buried under mounds of earth for protection and its connecting walkways, called 'cleanways', were scrupulously clean as dirt might cause that dreaded spark which could cause an explosion. ROF buildings were separated by vast distances, linked by their own rail or roads, in order to minimise the risk of an explosion setting up a chain reaction.

Filling was just about the most hazardous job. This was not merely because of the risk of explosions from a spark or vibration. Most of the work was done by hand and as health and safety procedures were in their infancy, women would often be ill handling toxic chemicals. Mabel Dutton worked at Risley Royal Ordnance Factory, near Warrington.

I was 19 years old. I was told I had to go to work on Group One. That group was nicknamed the Suicide Group on account of the many workers who had been blown up, killed, maimed or blinded. I didn't know it at the time but I would be working with highly explosive gunpowder for making detonators. On the first day, 12 of us from all over the place had to go into admin to be issued with a book of rules.

There were 3 working shifts – Mornings; Afternoons and Nights. Eleven went to Group Five Powder but I had to wait for a guide to take me to Group One.

It was then I noticed that she only had one hand and a finger missing off that. I asked her what had happened and she made up some story or other.

I later found out that she had had them blown off when she went to work on Group One.

I had to start on the afternoon shift which was 2pm until 10pm. I caught the bus from the Punch Bowl at Atherton to Leigh and then another bus from Union Street to Risley. Then we went on rickety wooden ones we called cattle trucks for about a mile to Group One. Outside, we had to leave our coats, shoes, bags, money, hairclips and anything metal in the Contraband Place and change into any old worn shoes, overalls and white turbans. I had bags, money, make-up, photographs and purse stolen many times. Even my own shoes.

On my first afternoon there, I was put in the Experimental Shop where we had to test the powder by weighing it on brass scales and sealing detonators one at a time. We had to wear goggles and leather gauntlets.

Sometimes the threat of disasters became all too real:

One day I was given a red box to carry with one person in front and behind carrying red flags walking along the clearways, taking them to be stored in

Women making shells for the Navy. Those who worked in munitions were among the best paid as their work was dangerous. All these women have their turbans firmly in place. (HMSO)

Munitions workers featured regularly in advertisements for make-up, such as this one promoting Miner's foundation.

magazines to be used later. I didn't know what I was carrying. There was a massive explosion and I dropped the box and was shocked to see a young woman thrown through a window with her stomach hanging out. Luckily the box, which contained detonators, did not explode or we would have had our legs blown off. I was sickened. When I got home, I said to my sisters Alice and Phyllis: 'I'm not going back there again.'

They laughed at me because they knew I had to.

We had a nice canteen with good food but the cups they served the tea in were usually cracked. We pushed them off the table to break them and get new ones. Sometimes, German planes came over dropping incendiary bombs and flares to light up the sky for the bomber planes. I had the job of banging on a big triangle to warn everyone to go into the shelter, then follow them in afterwards. There were always sheep in the shelters from the fields around the works. In the dark, it wasn't uncommon to sit on a sheep's back and when they ran off, I often found myself covered in sheep muck.

On a lighter note, we had Max Factor officials from Hollywood bring in some new pancake makeup and lipstick and tell us how to use it. It was all free and we were glad of it because we could only normally get face-cream and lipstick now and again. When we worked nights, some of us had a job to keep awake and someone gave us some pills that the RAF took to keep them awake on bombing missions. I had one and it kept me awake for days afterwards. I kept watch while the others had a nap.

There were Danger Building Inspectors who came round now and again to make sure we were wearing our goggles and we were warned of their approach by workers from other shops who used to whistle a certain tune. We were issued with white trousers and a coat with a mandarin collar and buttoned down front. We all had to wear caps or turbans. In the canteen we had concerts at lunchtime with artists from ENSA and sometimes the bosses would dress up and join in.

Mabel recalls one particularly shocking incident, and the personal effect it had on her.

If there was an explosion in the magazine or shops, we all had to go to the canteen for cups of tea and two cigarettes – which we had to pay for. The other girls used to argue over my two cigarettes as up to then, I didn't smoke. One day, a young girl came into our shop to sharpen a pencil and she had just gone back when there was such a bang. Everyone ran to see what it was except me. She had walked in through the door when the explosion occurred. She put her hands on the wall. One of them dropped off along with the fingers of the other hand. She was also blinded. As they wheeled her past on a stretcher, her naturally curly auburn hair was white and straight.

Seeing how shocked I was, the group nurse lit a cigarette and made me smoke it, supposedly to calm my nerves. She did the same the following day after another accident. It was the start of a lifelong habit.

Despite this very real danger, the frequent illnesses and injuries, the number of fatalities was actually comparatively small considering the work carried out in these factories. In fact, only 134 deaths were recorded in ROFs in total.

Unlike the aircraft factories under Beaverbrook, munitions factories introduced some of the most advanced management practices to maximise production. The three-shift days, mentioned by Mabel Dutton, compared favourably to 12-hour shifts worked elsewhere. Ordnance factories were so successful that by 1943, Britain had a surplus of shells and ROF workers were being laid off. Nellie Brook worked at another munitions factory, Thorp Arch.

I was in a self-contained room where no one else could go; it had two hatches at either side. This was where the detonators were filled with cordite for the guns. I don't have to tell you how dangerous and nerve racking it was and unhealthy – after a while your skin went yellow and you suffered with bad stomachs.

It happened to me when I had been there some time and was given permission to leave. I was off sick for only three weeks when I was called to the Labour Exchange. I was told my services were needed at A.W. Roe at Yeardon, where they made Lancaster bombers.

That was like something out of science fiction. To get there, we were taken out into the country. When you arrived you would never have thought there was a factory there, it was so well camouflaged; great big grass hillocks and once you went inside it was amazing. No windows, all these hundreds of people

Coughs and sneezes spread diseases

Trap the germs by using your handkerchief

Help to keep the Nation Fighting Fit

Before the war, the message had been not to spit on public transport. An improvement of sorts, then, in this jolly poster by H.M. Bateman. It is one of many on a similar theme.
(HMSO)

of both sexes all working away like ants all doing different jobs that finished up producing one of Britain's finest planes.

I must say the camaraderie was really good in that place – you got to know each other, even by sight, and there was a good canteen, first aid, offices . . . It was so huge that if you wanted to go to another section you went on a buggy. We worked on different shifts, days and nights.

While working there, I met my husband. He was on war work at another place so for quite a while we could only see one another at weekends. He came home as I set off to do my shift, so we kept a thick book where we would leave each other notes to keep us going.

ROYAL ORDNANCE FACTORY, HEREFORD

To :   Miss M.E. Cawthorne,

            "Audley"

                    Redhill Hostel,
                        Hereford.

    I am happy to inform you that for your devotion to duty on the
occasion of the explosions on 30th May, 1944 you have received
recognition.

    The Director General will announce particulars of the recognition
in the West Satellite Canteen at 4.30p.m. on Tuesday, 9th January, 1945.

    Seating accommodation has been reserved for you and for 2 relatives
or friends. Please arrange to be in your seats not later than 4.15p.m.

    The names of the 2 relatives or friends should be communicated by
you personally to Police Headquarters, War Department Constabulary,
R.O.F. Hereford not later than 5.0p.m. on Monday, 8th January, 1945.

    After the announcements, you are invited to tea with your 2 relatives
or friends in Central Office Mess Room.

    You are granted special leave with pay for your whole shift on
Tuesday, 9th instant.

                            R.D.qby Ovens
                            Superintendent,
                            R.O.F.Hereford.

3rd January, 1945
MVT

Munitions workers were much better treated than their colleagues in the aircraft factories. The first of these letters to Mona Cawthorne specifies paid leave from a whole (probably 8-hour) shift.

Anyway at the age of 25, I had my first little girl but even then, I worked until I was 8 months pregnant.

If speed was a theme of the 1930s, one of its most popular expressions was the craze for flying. Owning an aeroplane was beyond the means of most but people joined flying clubs which sprang up all over the country. But despite this widespread interest, when war broke out, pilots for the Royal Air Force were in short supply. Gerard d'Erlanger, a private pilot and banker, was on the board of British Airways. On 9 September 1939, he proposed the formation of the Air Transport Auxiliary to be made up of civilian pilots who would initially ferry people and messages in light aircraft, relieving the RAF of the work.

The *Daily Mail* in particular had exploited the flying craze throughout the 1930s, offering prizes for various flights. It made Amy Johnson the most famous pilot in England. A brilliant mechanic and pilot, she won £10,000 from the *Mail* in 1930, when she became the first woman to fly solo to Australia. But, although the most famous flyer in Britain was female, she and other women with more than 600 hours' experience piloting aircraft were admitted to the ATA only in the teeth of fierce opposition. As in so many other areas, necessity was the spur.

Mona Cawthorne, like her sisters Iris and Joyce, was in the Mechanised Transport Corps. Their duties included transporting munitions. The two letters featured here and on the facing page commend Mona for her bravery during an accident which occurred when she was on duty at ROF Hereford.

'They had to clear the ever-increasing number of aircraft from the factories and deliver them to the RAF squadrons, Fleet Air Arm bases or to the maintenance units. We sometimes flew the old ones away too,' said Diana Barnato Walker, Commodore of the ATA Association. 'Later on, as the Low Countries were released, we flew across the channel to the Group Support Units or the squadrons in Europe. We flew everyday in all weathers and without radio. We had to avoid flying into barrage balloons and sometimes got shot at by the enemy and, now and then, by our own side. We couldn't shoot back as our aircraft were not armed.' By 1944, she said, the ATA had 659 pilots, 108 of them women, from 28 nations. There were male and female flight engineers and about 3,000 back-up staff. Every aircraft flown by an RAF pilot had been flown by an ATA pilot first.

Betty Wilson was another of the ATA's female pilots:

You never felt a Spitfire or a Hurricane would go wrong – they were superb aircraft and they never failed. Getting lost, that was the biggest fear.

If you got lost, you were always told, 'circle and look for something'. But then the map would fall off your knee and there is only you and your two hands and you have to fly with one hand, but one got there.

Joan Hughes, Air Transport Auxiliary pilot, prepares to deliver a Short Stirling bomber to an operational bomber base. (Jonathan Falconer Collection)

I never did a flight when I wasn't scared rigid – I was always petrified. You'd look at the map and have your bit of string and say after take off, in three minutes I shall go to the right of a triangular wood. During take-off, you had to open the throttle – full throttle – get your wheels up, feather your aircraft and get your map out of your pocket.

By that time you'd hope the wood would be on the right hand side, because when you are travelling at the speed of a Spitfire, in about three minutes, if you are wrong, you are a long way wrong. And you only had enough fuel to get you to where you were going, so you can imagine it was scary.

I have thanked Julius Caesar for the Fosse Way more times than I can count because there was that wonderful road that went straight to the Cotswolds, as straight as a die, and you could follow it and it never let you down.

You had to fly on the left hand side of whatever you were following, and the odd thing was that if you looked down, you could see nothing but if you looked straight ahead, you could see it as if it were a pencil line right across the country.

There were more snags later when there were fears of invasion because the fields that were used as aerodromes were very much hidden. On one flight, I navigated what I thought was absolutely right and had come to where the aerodrome should have been and it wasn't there. It was just a field with cows. I circled in the approved style and suddenly from a barn at one end, RAF people came out and moved the cardboard cows, put up the windsock and one landed on this grass field but oh, can you imagine the relief?

ATA pilots were in constant demand, and Betty gained valuable experience on all sorts of aircraft.

Well, I flew lots of aircraft – Spitfires, Hurricanes, Tempests – all from factories to squadrons. The nicest squadron to get to was a Polish squadron because

Demand for pilots was such that the ATA could not ignore the many experienced women pilots who had learned to fly before the war.

they used to think we were absolutely wonderful. When we got to the British squadron, as sure as eggs they would say 'what the hell have you brought this for, we've got more Spitfires than we know what to do with'. But the Poles used to lift us off the wing and carry our parachutes for us – the English sergeants would see you drag your parachute and your overnight bag and anything else yourself.

Anyway, I carried on like that until I was sent to convert to twin engines. The man who was my instructor, he was an absolute bastard, he really was. When you taxi a single engine aircraft, you can't see forward at all and you have to keep one hand on the throttle and put the right brake on and turn this way, then the left brake on, and turn – it's the only way you can see forward. But in twins, you are up higher, you have two throttles and you taxi by using one throttle and then the other. This wretched man had a ruler and if I tried to turn by putting the brake on, he used to whack my hand with it.

So I came out of the pool again as a class three ferry pilot which meant flying all single and light twin engines. I never wanted to change to four-engined aircraft, because once you got on to fours you never flew anything else and it became really rather like driving a 'bus.

By the end of the war, the pilots of the ATA had flown 309,011 aircraft – 174 had died on duty, including Amy Johnson, reported missing over the Thames estuary in 1941.

CHAPTER 7

Making Do

CLOTHING

After the First World War, many widows bought sewing machines and supported their families by dressmaking from home. Fashions in the 1930s had featured elaborate, bias-cut garments which used masses of material to create flowing, draped lines in day and evening wear. Colours were bright and lively, and decorative finishing was expected, even on everyday garments.

By the end of this period, garments routinely featured pin tucks, pleats and other features all indicative of the high standards the garment industry had achieved. Synthetic textiles, especially artificial silk, which was derived from cellulose and invented earlier in the twentieth century, were increasingly popular. This and jersey knit fabrics especially meant that clothes could be more fitted to the lines and movement of the body. Men, women and children of all ages wore knitted cardigans, pullovers and sweaters.

Jewish tailors from Berlin and Vienna arrived in the East End of London in the 1930s, bringing with them graded patterns. The cutter made garments smaller or larger on the cutting table by adjusting the pattern accordingly. So the new sizing also reduced wastage. Until this point, off-the-peg clothes for women were marked as 'Maids' or 'Matrons', then 'SW', 'W' and 'WX' gave a guide to sizes.

Paris was still the centre of fashion for Europe and the USA in autumn 1939 and its fashion houses' attitude to the outbreak of war was perhaps comfortingly unreal. Paris had been the arbiter of taste and style in women's clothes since the nineteenth century and designers of women's clothing in all price ranges followed Paris styles, adapting haute couture for the mass market and adopting its preferences for the coming season, year after year. A few designers made reference to events outside the salons in their new designs; the Surrealist Elsa Schiaparelli's zip-fastening, one-piece 'alert' suit, in blue wool with 'damp-proof' (therefore, not waterproof) canvas boots was one such exception.

So the autumn collections went ahead as usual in 1939 and *Vogue* recalled that 'the cat-walks looked like an old-fashioned variety show, sporting dresses with hooped and hobble skirts and tight and shirred bodices, featuring every form of trimming from tassels to admiral's braid. Soft, smooth woollens, spongy crêpes, lavish velvets and miles of jersey were combined with pelt upon pelt of fur.' But the war began to affect what women wore, even at this early stage, as the London preference for puffed out, formal ball gowns disappeared almost immediately. *Vogue* approved, commenting that, 'it has taken a war to teach English women to wear restaurant clothes in a Continental manner'. Even as late as 1940, the Paris fashion houses were seen as still so vital to French exports that designers who had joined up were given two weeks special leave to finish their collections before returning to the front.

But by the time France was invaded, in June 1940, many of the best-known designers, such as Coco Chanel, had closed their salons in the capital for the duration of the war. Yet, one result of the German occupation was that Paris did not become subject to Allied wartime restrictions until it was liberated in 1944, so some designers were still able to work during the Occupation.

Leading British designers who had been employed by the Paris fashion houses soon found a new role working within the parameters set by British restrictions.

Born in 1925, Nancy Furlong was a schoolgirl in Newport, Monmouthshire (now Gwent), in September 1939. She recalls the school uniform she wore.

The new school year started and the winter uniform consisted of a black gymslip, white blouse, black and amber striped tie, black cardigan; black knickers and long black stockings held up by suspenders attached to a sleeveless vest reinforced with tape, called a Liberty bodice. We had black leather shoes, a black gaberdine raincoat topped with a black felt hat with a black and amber band holding the school insignia.

Summer uniform was a check cotton dress in either green, blue or pink, a blazer with insignia on the pocket, a straw hat with band and school insignia, and the depressing motto 'Nothing is good where better is possible.'

Immediately, we were told to continue wearing ankle socks during the winter because of the difficulty of obtaining long black stockings.

Long before the declaration of war, Government committees had discussed the need for rationing. Almost immediately, therefore, controls on timber were announced, which were quickly followed by restrictions on the use of textiles, including silk and its artificial equivalent, rayon, as well as leather, wool, cotton and flax. Although it was mainly home produced, wool was in short supply because the Government bought up as much as it could from domestic and overseas sources to provide material for uniforms. The demand for military outfits created a wool shortage on the civilian market, just as it had during and after the First World War. So it was no surprise when clothes rationing was introduced on Whit Sunday, 1 June 1941.

Clothes rationing was based on a points system. Anyone buying a garment had to surrender the correct number of coupons, the quantity reflecting the work and materials the garment demanded. At this stage, a woman's coat required fifteen coupons, a blouse needed five and a woollen dress eleven. Initially, sixty coupons were issued to each person in 1942 but, as with everything else, shortages increased as the war progressed so that in 1943, the clothing ration was cut to forty coupons; in 1944, it was forty-eight. At the same time, prices soared as shortages worsened. Coupons were needed for household linen too. 'When sheets wore thin in the middle, they were cut down the centre and the edges brought together and stitched to form a new middle.' Nancy Furlong remembers.

Ration book for clothing. At first, the system of replacing lost or stolen clothing coupons encouraged a thriving black market. In 1943, the Board of Trade said that 700,000 clothing coupon books had been stolen or lost, an indication of the scale of the problem. As a result, shopkeepers were not allowed to take loose coupons. Those in this book had to be stamped as they were used. This is a book from 1943–4, which replaced earlier ration books in another attempt to combat fraud.

Making do also meant looking after your clothes, and mobile laundries enabled families to still have clean clothes. This unit is in Portsmouth, where 65,000 out of the town's 70,000 houses had been damaged or destroyed. (HMSO)

Making do sometimes meant reclaiming what little you could from your wrecked home, like this woman carrying what remains of her possessions through ruins in London. (HMSO)

Inevitably, military styling and lines influenced fashions. From the late 1930s onwards, magazine advertisements depicted women modelling clothes *avec l'air militaire* alongside dashing young servicemen. Suits of short, square jackets with padded shoulders and shorter, knee-length skirts became increasingly popular as the war and rationing progressed.

Suits readily accommodated the now fashionable boxy silhouette, clearly more masculine than the line curving softly from shoulder to a high waist, which had been sought by women in the 1930s. Moreover, suits could be worn at any time and for any occasion, work or leisure: wartime weddings started the fashion for brides in two-piece suits. Trousers were also worn by women for all but the most formal occasions. They were very suitable for work in factories where all the female employees would wear trousers or one-piece overalls known as siren suits, the latter so-called because they could be pulled on quickly when an air-raid warning sounded.

Berets were popular with women and were at first worn puffed up. Before long, the practical necessity of tucking hair safely under berets or turbans created a style of its own for most women. Before the war, hats had been essential fashion accessories and were designed to match an outfit. Women owned several

This woman, measuring and cutting slates for re-use, epitomises wartime fashions in her trousers, short jacket, ankle socks and low-heeled 'sensible' shoes. (Kent Messenger Group)

handbags, hats, shoes and scarves in coordinating colours, patterns and styles. All that changed now as hats and headscarves became essentially practical items for keeping hair out of the way.

Short hair was fashionable with some, although many women still preferred to keep their hair long, but off the face. As the war drew to a close, women adopted the 'Victory Roll', a style in which the hair was rolled up tightly around the head and topped with a swept-up curl. Hair, like make-up, added a much needed dash of glamour and the popular wisdom was that it boosted morale for women themselves and the men around them. Bobby pins (hair grips) were very much prized.

Many hats were now home-made, especially knitted snoods and turbans. Home knitting was the patriotic duty of females of all ages. They made socks, balaclavas (with and without ear flaps!), scarves, squares for blankets, vests, sweaters and anything else that was needed, often getting together in knitting circles using wool supplied for the purpose by the WVS or other voluntary groups. The family's jumpers, vests and other items were knitted at home too. So it was not surprising that women took their knitting into shelters during air raids, to work and anywhere else they could manage a row or two.

High heels were now hopelessly impractical and generally unobtainable

A 'Making Do' classic – boleros and turbans were often made from recycled wool. A bolero was often used to smarten up a daytime outfit for evening wear, especially with the heavy necklace seen here.

so flat shoes, including the first wedge heels, became almost universal footwear for women. Leather was in short supply so synthetic uppers and soles made of wood or rubber became the norm, leading to clumpy shoes with short, wide heels and making clogs popular again.

Large handbags in all-purpose black, brown or other dark shades were popular, as were designs incorporating special compartments for the new essential accessory, the gas mask. With the family ration books, identification cards and other wartime paraphernalia to take with them, women simply had more to carry.

The 1930s fashions for animal fur and skins was another impractical dream in wartime so alternatives such as rabbit (unconvincingly disguised as '*lapin*', or in its dyed form, mystifyingly labelled 'sealine') were used. Synthetic and recycled materials imitated lizard, crocodile and snakeskin. Feathers were gathered from larger domestic birds and often used singly on hats.

As clothes became more plain and serviceable, so decoration was added with embroidery on a garment, elaborate hairstyles or make-up featuring bright red lips. Alongside the general restrictions, the Board of Trade announced the Utility scheme, which was to make the best use of raw materials for furniture and clothing. By this time, the purpose was not simply to avoid unnecessary use of precious resources, it was also to release textile and garment workers for other tasks and, by cutting garment production, to free up factory space for other work.

The Board of Trade launched Utility, with its famous CC41 logo, in 1941. The trademark was designed by Reginald Shipp and his brief was to 'design the double C so that the public should not recognise the symbols as such'. Within the Board of Trade, the symbol was referred to as 'the cheeses'. The 41 referred to the date of the scheme's creation and the term 'Utility' was coined by Alison McInnes, later Lady Peck, who was at that time secretary to Sir Laurence Watkinson at the Board of Trade.

The Civilian Clothing Order introduced Utility clothing to the public in 1942. During this year, each member of the London Society of Fashion Designers, which included such famous names as Hardy Amies, Norman Hartnell, Bianca Mosca, Worth, Digby Morton and Victor Stiebel, was asked to create four outfits. The resulting thirty-two costumes were pooled and the Board of Trade selected the most suitable top coats, suits, afternoon dresses and cotton overall dresses for mass production. This first Utility range was shown at the Board of Trade the following autumn, when *Vogue* remarked that, 'all women now have equal chance to buy beautifully designed clothes suitable to their lives and incomes. It is a

The famous 'two cheeses', symbolising the Utility scheme.

Three of the original thirty-two designs submitted to the Board of Trade in 1942 by the London Society of Fashion Designers. The straight-line, patch pockets and three buttons on the coat, the short military style jacket and shirt-waister style dress are all typical of the Utility clothing scheme, which these designs helped to launch. (HMSO)

revolutionary scheme and a heartening thought. It is, in fact an outstanding example of applied democracy.' From a design viewpoint, the restrictions of Utility, *Vogue* decreed, 'simply pare away superfluities'.

All garments produced under the scheme were quality and price controlled. They conformed to the Board of Trade's regulations for the scheme. These included a maximum of three buttons to a jacket, and a ban on heels more than 2 in high, peep-toe shoes, turned back cuffs and button-down pockets. Unnecessary decoration was not permitted and garments that could be 'mixed and matched', such as jackets suitable for day and evening wear, were encouraged. Material was kept to a minimum – bias cutting was out of the question.

With the annual issue of clothing coupons buying less and less, women needed no encouragement to 'Go Through your Wardrobe and Make Do and Mend', in the words of one poster of the day. The drive to Make Do and Mend meant re-using and adapting old garments rather than replacing them. A Board of Trade booklet, one of many official and unofficial publications, showed how to make a woman's skirt from a pair of man's plus-fours and a woman's top by knitting sleeves to add to a man's waistcoat.

Probably one of the best-known and least inspiring posters of the war promoting 'Make-Do and Mend'. (HMSO)

One of the most popular booklets of the wartime era, 'Make Do and Mend' covers everything from laundering to sewing, measuring to keeping moths away.

Nor was 'Make Do and Mend' confined to the family's own needs. 'Can you help others – for instance, by organising a group of women with some needlework skill and a little time, to repair the overalls of the local war workers? Ask the welfare or personnel departments of the factories if you can help', the Board of Trade urged. One common practice was for women to cut themselves a jacket and skirt from their husbands' dinner suits. Panels would be set into dresses, children's clothes made from adults' cast-offs. Sleeves would be short or completely absent. Beaded belts, cord and rope were used instead of elastic, which needed precious rubber and so was difficult to obtain.

Children had particular problems as they outgrew clothes and shoes quickly and were allocated some additional coupons to compensate in part for their additional needs. Girls with uniforms they had outgrown would offer them for sale to younger girls and, of course, no coupon exchange was involved in this or other secondhand clothes swapped or bought. The WVS clothing exchanges were essential to supplement the limited rations. At the end of 1942, older children were given extra clothing coupons. Younger children who were 5 ft 3 in or more in height or who weighed 7 stone 12 lbs or more were also to receive additional tokens.

Seams were let out, hems let down. Mothers sacrificed their own dresses to be cut down for their daughters. Nancy Furlong had her own particular dress problems.

A WVS clothing exchange. The clothing exchanges, especially good as a source of clothes for growing children, carried on long after the war had ended.

In my family, I was the only girl with three older and one younger brother so there was no larger clothing for me to grow into. My Mother would say, 'make it look as if it was meant' meaning when making necessary alterations, do it so that it looked like part of the original design. She was an excellent needlewoman.

Fabrics were not so easy-care as nowadays. Cotton was often lightly starched and ironed damp. Rayon and satin crêpe had to be ironed damp too. The rayon crêpe dresses had a nasty habit of shrinking to indecent proportions should one get caught in a summer storm.

Wool had to be carefully washed by hand. You had to give coupons for new wool and I spent some of mine on enough wool to knit a pair of school gloves, which I did to pass the time in air-raid shelters at school. They were knitted on four needles and unfortunately I never managed to get the fingers in the right places. They ended up as fingerless mittens!

When Nancy finished school she had more clothing difficulties.

I left school in 1941 and went to a private business to learn shorthand and typing. The school uniform having been discarded, I had to make do with whatever clothing was available. My only coat was a dark green emerald colour with plaid trim on collar and cuffs but it was only meant for spring and summer wear and in the winter the wind blew right through it. Combined with only ankle socks, whatever the weather, it meant that I was always cold and suffering from chilblains.

Shortly after this I started work at the local Income Tax Office and I rode to and fro on an old bicycle. Fortunately we got hold of some knitting wool and Mother made me two pairs of knee length socks held up by elastic under a turn over top which kept me much warmer.

Wooden clog-type shoes could be obtained without coupons. They were very noisy and I could always recognise my friend who wore them coming along the corridor at work. It was this friend who persuaded me to volunteer for the Women's Auxiliary Air Force (WAAF). Her persuasion combined with the fact that my brother Lyndon was in the RAF and I thought that the grey-blue uniform would suit me better than that awful khaki the ATS wore!

Knitwear could be made from odds and ends of wool recycled from old garments. This popularised multi-coloured designs, especially as it saved the wearer's valuable clothing coupons. Women's magazines and booklets offered patterns and advice on re-using everything from vegetables and teas for dyes to making a teddy bear out of an old car rug.

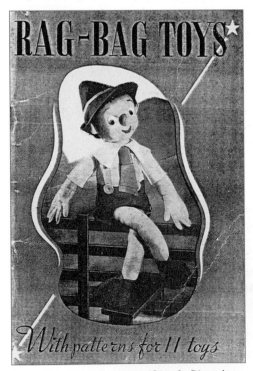

'Rag-Bag Toys' featuring 'Simple Simon' on the cover, who is made from old stockings, an abundance of which would be needed to make the stuffed toys in this booklet. The inside back cover has a fold-out paper pattern.

Nylon stockings, which came onto the European market in 1939, just as war broke out, disappeared again to become the stuff of dreams, until American GIs brought them over later in the war. Stockings, even silk and artificial silk, were very difficult to find so women painted their legs with a special preparation. 'It was not that easy to get an even effect and you needed someone to draw the back seam on with a brown eyebrow pencil. I found that the colour rubbed off on to your clothing so didn't use it that often,' says Nancy Furlong. Not that cosmetics were easy to find. Olive Owens remembers that in the absence of proper make-up: 'For foundation, we put on a light layer of cold cream with calamine lotion dabbed over it.

We would let that dry and put powder over the top. It might have looked ludicrous by today's standards but it looked quite good to us then.'

Underwear presented specific problems for women especially – even before the war, many men did not routinely wear underpants and vests and socks were often home-produced. Metal for fastenings, like elastic, was in short supply and often of poor quality. Collectors of vintage clothing today find that metal hooks and eyes used on wartime lingerie are more prone to rust than that of the pre-war equivalents. Utility underwear was usually peach in colour, although pink was available too. Younger women wore 'French knickers', with side button fastenings instead of elastic, a style that had been popular in the 1930s. Camisoles, bras and underslips were easier to find than 'Roll-ons'. 'Roll-ons' were elasticated foundation garments that incorporated suspenders and were anchored in place by stockings – so were doubly impractical in wartime.

Artists, designers and illustrators played their part with a range of distinctive wartime-related textile designs. In 1941, the Cotton Board was given a Government subsidy to commission a series of fabrics. Duncan Grant, Ben Nicholson and Graham Sutherland were among the contributors, as was the cartoonist Fougasse, whose 'Careless Talk' series of posters was printed on Jaqmar silk. The following year, Jaqmar's Arnold Lever produced a series of propaganda prints. They were made into aprons, dresses and blouses designed by Bianca Mosca, and featured slogans such as 'The Navy's Here', 'Home Guard' and 'Dig for Victory'. Brooches and other jewellery in 'V for Victory' designs were popular decoration and deemed morale boosters.

War ended not a moment too soon for the fashion conscious. Military styling, padded shoulders and an emphasis on simplicity had run their course and women wanted glamour again. Christian Dior's 'New Look' collection of 1947 (he called it the 'Corelle') was an exclusive but influential fulfilment of this wish. His clothes were extravagantly cut, shaped and draped. The long skirts needed yards of material. Looking back to those ludicrously anachronistic collections of Paris in autumn of 1939, it is easy to see how Dior's 'New Look' recalled the romantic, full-skirted and extravagant gowns that had influenced Britain before being rudely interrupted by the war.

However, like the nylon stockings less than a decade before, the 'New Look' was an ideal to be sought out and dreamed of. As shortages worsened after the war, clothing stayed on ration and was even more difficult to obtain for a while. Clothing coupons were issued until September 1948. The Utility scheme continued until 1952, albeit with fewer and fewer restrictions so that by the time it ended it was little more than a means of controlling the prices of certain garments by giving exemption from purchase tax. But, obviously, clothing was not the only thing in short supply. It was important to preserve and use food economically, as it was other raw materials.

FOOD

In 1939, the Government Food Department drew up the National Register as a prelude to issuing everyone with ration books. Different regulations were to be applied to different groups of people, reflected in the colours of the ration books.

Ration book for food. Every adult and child in the family had a ration book, with children's food allowances depending on their ages. By 1943, when this book was issued, furniture was also rationed.

The Adult book was a cream colour, the Child's book, green, and the Junior book, blue – children were allowed orange juice and cod liver oil, and younger children got extra milk. Butter, bacon and ham were the first foods to be rationed. Sugar joined the list very soon after, followed by meat, the latter rationed by value and not weight. Production of non-essential items was restricted from May 1940, by which time the Food Department had been renamed the Ministry of Food and was headed by Lord Woolton.

Madge Parnell worked in her mother-in-law's grocery shop and describes how complicated her job became with the introduction of rationing.

Our shop was on the corner of a street in Northampton, an area with lots of children so we were always busy. Customers had to register as we were only allowed enough rations for registered customers plus extra for members of the services on leave. So it was a full-time job keeping the records. I used to do all the paperwork, which meant a lot of forms to fill in, coupons to be counted and then taken to the Food Office. It was a full day's job itself as the office was always full of people. And they were always making alterations to the rations, it was a nightmare.

We were allowed to sell vegetables and had balance scales with various weights – the largest was 7 lbs. We were not allowed to sell ice cream. Bread was supplied neither sliced nor wrapped. It was weighed by the inspectors from the Ministry of Food. If it was underweight, we were fined – I never could work that one out!

Madge also recalls how difficult the situation was for their customers.

Mothers used to come in the shop on Mondays for their rations when the goods were delivered to us and some would come back in on Fridays hoping we hadn't cut the coupons – you couldn't blame them for trying.

Elsie, my mother in law, was very kind. We both had to go without lots of things as she often gave our rations to the local children.

The shop was a short distance from a school and the police station so we always had plenty of customers. Des O'Connor was a local boy then and he would come in every day hoping for sweets. He had a way with him in those days as well.

Cigarettes were a pain for us. We tried to keep them for our regular customers, especially the police who were very good to us.

When the siren went, we grabbed the money drawer – no fancy tills then – and anything else we could and scuttled across the road to the school boiler room, where everyone went. We had tea and coffee – only 'Camp' coffee in those days – and everyone brought something with them. There we would stay until the all-clear.

My son Michael was born in February 1944 and on Fridays, I used to put him in his pram and take him with me when I went to fetch the bacon rashers for the customers. It was no good getting the bacon in the shop on Mondays – they would have eaten it as soon as they bought it because things were very scarce by then.

Certainly the introduction of rationing ensured that a nutritious if not always appetising diet was available for all, although the shortages increased and so rations were regularly reduced as the war went on. Tea, jam, milk and cheese were added to the list. Rationing did not prevent shortages and at other times, goods might suddenly appear briefly. Women became so used to queuing that it became a national habit, if one saw a queue, to join it and find out later what was on offer. Bananas and other imported fruit all but disappeared. Chocolate and sweets, if available at all, were often of poor quality.

Alongside rationing went the drive to increase home food production and, as with clothing, women were not short of advice via official and unofficial booklets, radio programmes and lectures about making the best of available resources. Some of this was good practical information; some was little more than wishful thinking. As women tried to keep the family fed with dried eggs, jams and tarts made from all manner of vegetables, the children of the family were less convinced that Treacle Toffee Carrots and eggless, fatless cakes were as good as the prewar alternatives. Carol Burton was a child living in Spalding, Lincolnshire, during the war: 'My mother used to pick up any sugar-beet that had been dropped from a cart and boil it for hours in a large saucepan over an open fire. The result was a syrup which could be used to

'Kitchen Parade'. The daily menus featured in this 1941 publication already show a disturbing fondness for cabbage and beetroot soup. In the preface, popular author Richard Llewellyn says, 'My friend Diener left Vienna and the Three Hussars Restaurant because of Hitlerites and hooliganism.'

sweeten cooked fruit, but the all pervading smell was so sickly that food seemed less appealing, even in those days of acute shortage. I remember despairing of my mother. We had a very small ration of butter which I loved, and a rather larger ration of margarine which in those days tasted abominable. My mother insisted on beating the two together, though in my mind this practice entirely spoiled the butter without making the margarine any more palatable.'

Communal Feeding Centres, later British Restaurants, were set up and served cheap and healthy meals, using food that was not rationed. On the other hand, the Dig for Victory campaign emphasised the need to boost home-grown food – already, every available piece of private and public ground had been turned into

Communal sleeping arrangements such as the large public shelter in Stoke Newington seen here gave accommodation to one in twenty-five Londoners during the Blitz. Communal feeding schemes ensured people could eat and food was prepared with minimum fuel and wastage. (HMSO)

allotments, including gardens. Nothing was thrown away and scraps left over would be collected street by street in large bins for pig food. However, not every plan worked in the way expected. Margaret Stevenson's dad had a butcher's shop, in Walthamstow, east London: 'We lived a few miles away in Chingford. We had a goose and he fattened it up for us. I had to take it home on the bus in my shopping bag and it kept sticking its head out. We were going to kill it and eat it for Christmas but then it started to lay eggs – enormous ones that filled the pan. We could not bring ourselves to kill it by the time Christmas came, although it died eventually because it got an egg stuck in its bottom.'

The house that Margaret lived in was a typical suburban semi, with a garden and garage. 'We kept lots of animals. The garage had rows of cages with rabbits, which we kept for eating. We had ducks in the garden too. We kept chickens. You could exchange your egg ration for chicken feed [rationed because it was imported] so we did that and we fed the chickens on potato peelings too. We had a lot of eggs and we used to sell some to the grocer's for 6 shillings a dozen. And Bill, my husband, was very good at gardening so we grew lots of vegetables and fruit ourselves. We never went short of food – we were very well supplied one way or another.'

Mass feeding at workplace canteens was a practical way to use resources. Bridget Bolwig worked for Sainsbury's, in an occupation quickly assigned 'reserved' status.

I had a wonderful boss who was awarded an OBE at the end of the war and the Department was later increased by a retired admiral's widow who, for industry, enthusiasm and charm, took top prize!

Our task was to set up in the basements of Stamford House (Sainsbury's HQ), a staff canteen capable of serving 1,000 meals, drinks and snacks, as well as looking after four smaller canteens in the vicinity of Blackfriars, where we had to keep happy the staffs of the bacon factory, the main factory, the garage and the Directors' dining room. Only the main canteen was open for breakfasts and suppers but all of them served coffees, snacks and lunches, day in, day out.

I was responsible for advising about equipment as I had experience of large scale catering and my first job was to recommend which of the three possible 'Hobart' electric mixers the Firm should buy.

Bridget found her work hard, but it had its rewards.

It was fairly hand to mouth at the beginning. The Blitz was on and breakfast staff had to be accommodated at nights for a crack of dawn start. The cashdesk and the cash register were major problems; early on, before a suitable cashier could be appointed, I had to do a few early turns on that too and, once, was unwise enough to ride down on my bike – forgetting what a long, long uphill haul awaited me at the end of the day with, as likely as not, my boyfriend arriving dirty and exhausted in the middle of the night, after fighting fires in the blitzed East End.

Anyway, the canteen was a terrific success and we became the showpiece of the Ministry of Food, demonstrating what could be done to make a grubby old basement a cosy eatery in the battered surroundings of Blackfriars.

On top of all that, the three of us took care of the 'catering establishments' as they were called of the approximately 650 branches of J. Sainsbury in the – roughly – south-east and Midlands. This meant endless calculations of ration allowances and points allowances, and ferreting out meatless and sugarless recipes – rather wearying – but it was a happy time all in all. We all got on together and after all, the food-producing workers had to be fed!

The WVS, Women's Institutes and other groups produced pamphlets and gave lectures on food preparation. Marjorie Goodliffe was a demonstrator:

I had been a housecraft teacher at Boots Day Continuation School, employed by Nottingham City Education Authority until I married in March 1939. Married women were not employed by the authority so of course, I was living at home, fully occupied, keeping house and looking after my husband!

In January 1940, the new housecraft organiser called at the house to say that a teacher who was to take a women's class at a local school that afternoon had been taken ill so could I take the demonstration?

Although I had my husband in bed with flu, I went off and took the class. The organiser sat through it, complimented me and arranged for me to take further classes.

As you can guess, I was soon fully employed, earning Technical Pay as I had done at Boots. I had to cook in the mobile canteen. You can imagine cooking for 200 in somewhere the size of a caravan! Coal fired boiler and copper. No hotplate. The procedure was to start at 8am and cook the dinner, have our dinner at 11.15am, then serve the children and the staff. In the afternoon, they had lessons on the theory of dietetics and kitchen management. The catering officers would usually give them a couple of talks, too. The idea was that they could go across with the mobiles when a European landing was made. I was also taken to their regional headquarters somewhere in Derbyshire to talk on similar topics to about 80 men who might go over with the first troops.

You can imagine starting with about six fresh women each month, but I had three regular local women all the time who also did the washing up after dinner and so on.

In Britain, nobody actually starved and nobody quite went unclothed during the shortages of wartime and the immediate post-war era. Much of the public advice and strategies on making do were very sound and the diet forced on the population was in fact a healthy one. But the lack of choice in food, as in clothing, meant that people wanted ice-cream, sweets, bananas, cakes and butter. So, after the war, although people knew what was good for them, they had lost interest in vegetables, even if they were home grown.

CHAPTER 8

Arts and Entertainment

Developments in printing and publishing, not least the introduction of paperbacks popularised by Allen Lane at Penguin Books, meant that for the first time a wider world of good quality literature was available to an eager audience in the 1930s. Books were as popular as ever in wartime, despite shortages of paper, which simply encouraged shorter novels. And while prices for theatre and, especially, cinema seats rocketed as the tax on each was put up, books remained exempt through the entire war.

Poster and commercial art was at its height and some of the best-known illustrators of the time were commissioned to design the posters calling on the nation's women to volunteer for the ATS or ARP or the Women's Land Army. Usually depicting up-to-the-minute hair styles, make-up and clothes, one typical poster shows a part-time factory worker punching Hitler on the nose. The caption reads 'A good afternoon's work'.

As the war progressed, women featured more and more prominently in their new roles demonstrating independence and capability. So impressed were British propagandists by the example set by Russian women that their images appeared frequently. A poster issued jointly by the Ministry of Labour and the Royal Society for the Prevention of Accidents showed a woman wearing a headscarf above the caption

> Cover Your Hair for Safety
> Your Russian Sister Does.

The hammer and sickle is helpfully placed in the corner of the almost completely red poster, should anyone fail to get the point that the Russians were now our friends.

The 1942 film *Mrs Miniver* is still one of the best-known war films of the time. It was an enormous success in the USA, but in Britain, the heroine's larder and wardrobes must have seemed very full. More realistic depictions of British life were seen in *Millions Like Us*, which appeared the following year and was directed by Frank Launder and Sydney Gilliat. As munitions workers it featured the actresses Patricia Roc, married to an airman played by Gordon Jackson, and Anne Crawford, who wins over the gruff factory foreman, played by Eric Portman.

Women were increasingly depicted as practical, down to earth and capable. Celia Johnson was a role model for middle-class women with serving husbands

Don't Fence Me In. *Hollywood meant escapism and this film featured two GIs (Robert Hutton and Dane Clark) who met Joan Leslie while on leave at the canteen, before going to fight in New Guinea. All the film's profits went to war charities and, with a wonderful line up of songs, it was an enormous success.*

and suffered gamely as Noel Coward's wife in the British hit, *In Which We Serve*. Those who moaned were usually the ones who died later in the film, usually in an air raid – that may be coincidence but it looks suspiciously like propaganda too.

Cavalcanti's 1942 film *Went the Day Well?* has a predominantly female cast. Produced by Ealing Studios and based on a story by Graham Greene, it emphasises the need for everyone to be prepared and to be able to act with necessary brutality against invaders and fifth columnists. The German army is held at bay by Land Girls Thora Hird and Elizabeth Allen, with their rifles; the lady of the manor, Marie Lohr, throws herself on a grenade to save local children. The village postmistress, played by Muriel George, kills a German soldier with an axe, sobbing as she does so to remind audiences of the difference between Nazi sadism and British expediency; the vicar's daughter, Valerie Taylor, calmly shoots the traitor she once loved.

The tension between American and British troops, particularly where women were concerned, was a frequent topic for films. It was addressed directly in *A Matter of Life and Death* (1943), and later in *A Canterbury Tale*, both produced by the Archers company of Michael Powell and Emeric Pressburger.

Nurses were reminded of their duty in *The Lamp Still Burns* (1943), in which Rosamund John chooses her career over love and marriage to Stewart Granger – nurses were not allowed to work if they married. Many British films of this time include sub-plots that emphasise the importance of women carrying on after the usually heroic death of menfolk, especially to look after the children.

As peace became simply a matter of time, other themes dominated the screens. The impact of war on marriage was the subject of *Waterloo Road* (1944) in which married soldier John Mills goes absent without leave to confront Stewart Granger, who has seduced his wife, Joy Shelton. This film marked the beginning of the post-war British realist style of film-making, which led to *Saturday Night and Sunday Morning* (1960).

Television, in its early infancy when war was declared, was shut down for the duration, so the radio was the only mass medium for news and entertainment. Everyone listened to the BBC news bulletins and other programmes such as the *Brains Trust, It's That Man Again* (ITMA) and, in the factories especially, *Music While You Work.*

A wartime cartoon by David Langdon about going to the cinema during the black-out.

CEMA (the Council for Education in Music and the Arts) was formed in 1940 to encourage the arts in wartime. Its activities were centred around classical concerts, art exhibitions, touring theatre companies – most notably the Old Vic, led by Sybil Thorndike – opera and ballet. The 1942 Humphrey Jennings film, *Listen to Britain,* helped popularise Dame Myra Hess as the enduring image of this great wartime demand for 'higher' art. Her lunchtime concerts from the National Gallery in London – by now stripped of its paintings – offered cheap tickets and were always sold out.

Of course, for much of the time, people made their own entertainment. It was often an opportunity to raise money for the War Effort and to put on a show for the forces. Nancy Furlong belonged to a dancing class from the age of five until she was eighteen.

We gave charity shows, took part in competitions and entertained the troops. We were 'Belle Cleverley and her Tiny Tots'. For these shows we wore costumes mainly made by our mothers. Crêpe paper featured a lot but it is a mystery to me still how they managed to find enough materials. One song we did was 'I like a nice cup of tea in the morning . . .'. So Belle Cleverley wrote to the boss of Lyons Corner Houses and he loaned enough costumes from his Nippies [waitresses]. My other contribution to entertaining the troops was as a second violinist in the Civil Defence Orchestra. The men wore dark suits, white shirts and black ties, often the bow type. The ladies wore their smartest day dresses. I think the soldiers only came because they got a cup of tea and free cigarettes.

Dancing was as popular as ever and everyone – civilians and members of the forces – would jitterbug, waltz and conga at one of the many hundreds of local dances taking place on any night of the week, raids permitting. Mary Archer recalls some of her evenings: 'In 1943, I was at Headington, in a small branch of the bank where I worked. The Oxford and Bucks Light Infantry were at Cowley barracks and the officers used the branch. I had many a good evening at the Mess dances – escorted to and from home – and got very friendly with one captain at this time. Sadly, he was sent overseas and forgot me! The American 2nd Army were at the Churchill Hospital, which they built – and one soldier brought me sweets and once a pair of stockings.'

Doreen Perkins' teenage social life was also typical of many girls: 'If there was a dance in our village, my Mum used to chaperone us. My older sister and I also went into Peterborough regularly. There was a crossroads on the way and we'd wait there until the Americans came along. My sister would wave her white handkerchief at them to flag them down and we would all get in their Jeep and that's how we got to dances in the town. There was an army camp at Yaxley as well and if we went to dances there, the soldiers at the camp would walk us home and then they would walk back to the camp.'

Jazz and swing music made way for deeply sentimental tunes which reflected everyday wartime concerns, such as 'Goodnight, wherever you are'. Two of the most popular stars were the singer and actress Gracie Fields, who appeared in numerous films set in factories during the late 1930s and early 1940s, and Vera Lynn, the 'Forces Sweetheart'. Lynn's deep, warm voice suited these romantic ballads perfectly and she

'We'll Meet Again' – Vera Lynn's finest hour.

broadcast every Sunday to troops overseas, not, initially, with much official approval. The half-hour programme, *Sincerely Yours, Vera Lynn*, consisted of songs and messages to and from the troops and their families at home. The official view was that if the men thought too much about their families and girlfriends, it would affect morale badly.

ENSA was set up to provide entertainments for the forces and others involved in war work. The initials stood for Entertainments National Service Association, though it was popularly known as 'Every Night Something Awful'. ENSA was made up of all kinds of professional entertainers. At first, women with little or no theatrical experience volunteered for ENSA in large numbers, attracted by the comparative glamour of a life on stage compared to working in a factory. Robina Hinton was an established professional in the theatre in the 1930s and worked with ENSA throughout the war years.

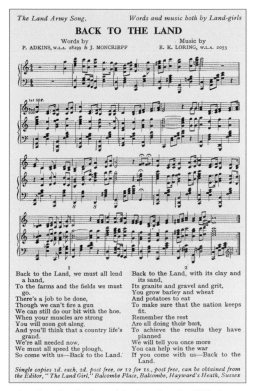

Another fundraiser, this time for the WLA Benevolent Fund, 'Back to the Land' was written by two members of the Land Army.

Deferment was granted to women on call-up for the war if they could prove that they had three years of work for known theatre managements. I was able to get this 'open-ended'. I worked in the musical theatre and forces shows.

ENSA headquarters was in the Drury Lane Theatre using the backstage area and the stage for rehearsals, offices, wardrobe etc. Everyone working in a unit had to have a green identity card for access to the bases. You could be asked to play anywhere, within the British Isles including the Scottish island of Iona and Northern Ireland.

Some of the crossings could be a little hairy. To go overseas you had to have a uniform based on army uniform, passport and medical. I was to due to go down to France but failed the medical with a tooth abscess. Lucky for me – my unit came back with the Dunkirk men, in a cattle boat, and was bombed all the way.

The units covered all types of entertainment from classical music to plays to concert party and variety.

The Hintons had to adapt to working in many different situations and conditions:

As Reg Hinton, my husband, was C3 (medically unfit), and not eligible for call-up he decided to work in the blitzed and most dangerous places, as a priority.

So we worked in Dover when it was being shelled and bombed at the same time – and where the stage gave way so I fell through to my waist; the East End theatres; London; Birmingham and Manchester, all the main cities.

We called the act Hinton and Robina and later, when we were established, 'The Hintonis'. I either worked in the Garrison Theatre or revue type shows or variety using a single dance act. Latterly we did the normal double act we did in the variety theatre.

ENSA units could be any size, depending on where they were working. The smallest would travel by lorry and the lorry would provide the stage or up to the biggest units which travelled by coach and played to the big bases and the garrison theatres, which had excellent facilities. Lodgings could be in private houses or hotels that had been taken over. Pubs, forces barrack type hostels, or wonderful large houses on large private estates.

RAF bases were always difficult for variety acts using high apparatus as their ceilings were always low.

The Navy was always a favourite. Once, we were working a navy landbase on what had been a holiday camp. My work involved rolling around the floor a bit and usually I checked the stage but had not bothered on this occasion – the Navy was always so very clean. This time they had slipped up. When I came off stage I was standing looking at my dirty self when a rating came up to me, stood smartly to attention and announced, 'Madam, your bath is ready.' That was the most

Robina Hinton, third right, wearing the long dress with the jewelled waist, with the cast of a wartime show.

wonderful bath of the war. In the Wren officers' quarters, gorgeous hot water, smooth soap – not like our rations – soft towels. I could have stayed there for hours.

There were many different aspects to a job with ENSA, as Robina discovered.

When we were on the bases we were expected to go to the officers' or sergeants' messes after the show and this was usually very enjoyable. At all times, our behaviour was monitored and any bad mark could send you home.

The length of time you were with a unit could be anything – from three to six months as once out, they tended to stay out for a while. The pay was five pounds a week for chorus, solo artistes eight pounds a week, top stars ten pounds a week and all keep 'found'.

Working in the West End could mean theatre, large floor show (at this time all the big restaurants round Piccadilly had lavish floor shows) or night clubs again around the Piccadilly or Regent Street areas. These latter were sought after bookings as they were underground and artistes felt fairly safe.

I was working at the Coliseum in London and we were asked if we would go to an army unit 'somewhere on the south coast' to give a show. Off we went and the atmosphere in the camp was unusual, the audiences barely wishing to applaud. We slunk back to London, convinced we had given a really bad show. It wasn't until some considerable time later that I discovered our audiences had been men who had been Dunkirk refugees. No wonder they were in no mood for light entertainment – their faces are still with me today.

Shortages took their toll on performances, as in every other area of life. However, Robina became adept at 'Making Do'.

Some ENSA shows were not so good but these were in a minority taking into account the circumstances we had to deal with. My husband remarked that some of the poorer units could be blamed on the producers who put in what he called 'pub and club' acts, not true professionals. As my husband, many years my senior, had started his variety performing in the late 1920s, I think he knew the score.

There was no comparison between ENSA and civilian theatre. In ENSA, you were a parcel. Taken, put down, then picked up and moved on. Civilian theatre was entirely your own responsibility.

Costumes just had to be contrived and we used stuff from secondhand shops, cut down and re-used. A new production could apply for an extra allowance of clothing coupons but there was a limit to these. Sequins soon became scarce so I went into a big suppliers and bought a huge amount. I had one costume pre-war which was like a complete modern-day Lycra skin, covered all over in sequins hand sewn, which had to be replaced almost every performance. When I started ENSA I persuaded the wardrobe to give me a costume in place of the sequinned one and they came up with a (brief) silk leotard and a chiffon long split overdress. This the troops certainly approved of.

We got a small caravan and a car when we found that variety people could get coupons for petrol through the Showman's Guild but these were severely rationed to the exact mile so care had to be taken not to take a wrong turning. My husband coasted down all the hills.

The ENSA tag (Every Night Something Awful) never bothered us. Professionals could always make an audience enjoy themselves. Troops were easy to work to.

Shortages were worse after the war and a visit to southern Ireland was eagerly sought because you would be able to have a banana, lots of butter and things like that. Heaven. Customs didn't usually bother us as we all travelled with our stage pictures, used for the front of the house, on the top, inside our trunks. But on one bill we worked over there, one of the acts had done a lot of coupon-free clothes shopping, including a long fur coat. We all said, 'How will you get on in customs?' Well, she turned up with the coat on and an outrageous hat. Nothing was said.

The nostalgic image of relentlessly cheerful Cockneys singing songs in the shelters during air raids has been rather overdone, post-war, but it is true that many people made their own entertainment for much of the time.

A popular way to raise morale was through pin-up competitions. Sheila Ashton (née Wigham) won the hearts of several airmen when she entered a local newspaper competition with this photograph: 'A lot of them used to write to me but the letters had to go through the local police station or the Mayor first!'

The Government initially closed down all theatres, cinemas and other places of entertainment at the outbreak of the war but soon appreciated the importance of an escape from the realities of wartime life to morale. It also realised especially, a long time after Dr Goebbels had set such a magnificent example, the importance of cinema as a means of propaganda. But although cinemas drew large audiences, it was the glamour and escapism offered in Hollywood films that had people queuing round the block. *Gone with the Wind*, released in 1939, was one of the most popular films throughout the war. Others, equally as well liked, were lavish musicals such as *Meet Me in St Louis* (1944) with Judy Garland and tear-jerkers such as *Random Harvest* (1942).

Wartime meant that women and teenagers who might otherwise have been more closely chaperoned became used to going out alone, or with friends their own age. This independence, while not an entirely new wartime phenomenon, was far more commonplace than it might otherwise have been and it continued well into the post-war era.

CHAPTER 9

Family Life and Getting Back Together

During the Second World War, although family life went on, it was inevitably very different from peacetime, wherever one lived. The entire nation was a resource and everyone felt the impact.

The evacuation of children from cities at risk from bombing made enormous changes to home life, for the evacuees, their parents and their foster parents. Carol Burton of Spalding, Lincolnshire, remembered the evacuees she met.

They came to us from the Grimsby docklands area and brought to our rural community a seemingly alien culture. They were tough, sophisticated and deprived.

We had half-day schooling for a time, so that the incoming evacuated school, complete with teachers, could use our building in the afternoon. One woman with a very small boy was billeted with us for a time, but, regrettably the two families were not compatible. Neither seemed to have any notion of 'how the other half lived'. I am not proud of that episode, though I do remember the unhappy disruption in our home.

Not all the 'evacuees' Carol came into contact with were children.

Later, we had a very different evacuee. She was a naive, refined, young woman, married at the early age of seventeen to a serving army officer and living for weeks in underground shelters in Plymouth. When she came to us she was blissfully unaware that she was infested with lice and had to be told what they were. I remember one part of the treatment was dowsing her hair in paraffin, followed by the wrapping of her head in a towel for many hours. However, my mother managed to cure the problem.

When our spare room was not occupied by evacuees, a succession of soldiers occupied it instead, from a humble corporal to high ranking officers. One officer smuggled a woman in overnight, which scandalised my parents and assorted neighbours. I didn't understand what he had done wrong, and no one explained. One illustrious Major was discovered to be an earl in civilian life, much to my mother's gratification.

In just about every war, the heightened danger and, especially, the ever-present threat of sudden death affect people's sexual behaviour, with the inevitable increase in illegitimate births. The First World War was no exception to this rule, nor was the Second, although overall the decline in the birth rate accelerated. There was still a stigma attached to being an unmarried mother and pregnancy out of wedlock also led to wartime weddings. But not always. During the Second World War in Britain, one-third of all births were illegitimate.

Alice Ewing met one single mother on a maternity ward in December 1943. 'We were snowed in so the ARP team were called after the only ambulance had broken down in the snow. The ARP people thought it was a joke at first but my butcher was in that particular team – I'd fainted in his shop – so he knew it wasn't. Anyway, they got me to New Cross Hospital in Wolverhampton and put me in a bay with just one other mother. The nurse came along and said some people had walked past saying 'that's another one of those unmarried mothers' – they were put in the bay, separate from the married women. The nurse put them right but my husband was furious and so I was moved into a ward. But the girl already in the bay, she really was an unmarried mother. She said to me, "Do you want this baby?" but I said no, that I had three of my own to look after.'

There were plenty of opportunities to meet and socialise. Factory workers, Land Girls and other 'mobile women' were often billeted in their hundreds or even thousands in small industrial towns or villages, in hostels or private homes. Factory and forces dances, bringing hundreds of people together at a time, were regular events in the days before television.

Allied troops gave an exotic and attractive twist to wartime romance. GIs from the USA were as popular with British women as they were unpopular with the British men who called them, 'Overpaid, oversexed and over here.' GIs received on average seven times more pay than their British counterparts – and had ready access to the chocolate, chewing gum and stockings that was the stuff of dreams for the British by the time the Americans arrived in 1943. Black GIs were for many the first black people they had ever met.

Another wartime tradition that the Second World War upheld was an increase in prostitution. So brisk was business for London prostitutes that they offered sex fully clothed and standing up, against lamp-posts during the black-out. Known popularly as 'Piccadilly Warriors', they would shout, 'Hey Yank, quick, Marble Arch style!' The House of Commons debated the problem, not least because of the pedestrian congestion this caused in parts of the capital.

Unsurprisingly, rates of venereal disease soared among the American troops – it was six times that of the rate for British troops on home duty. A public awareness campaign was launched, despite official reluctance, but with widespread public support. The rate of venereal disease among British troops had shown a similar increase at the start of the war, and as time passed, increasingly frank and even lurid poster campaigns and leaflets warned against the disease. One result of all this was that by the end of the war, the British were much better informed about sex than they might otherwise have been.

Mrs Joyce Crang was three years old when her mother became a warden in a hostel for the Women's Land Army. 'We had another, empty hostel next door,

Patron:
HIS MAJESTY THE KING.

President:
HER MAJESTY THE QUEEN.

Chairman of the Council:
H.R.H. THE DUKE OF GLOUCESTER, K.G.

Chairman of the Executive Committee:
The Hon. Sir ARTHUR STANLEY, G.B.E., C.B., M.V.O.

This is to Certify that

Mrs Kathleen Mitchell

has completed one year's **War Service** from _3·9·39_ to _1·5·41_
as duly certified, in accordance with the regulations under the auspices of the
Society in connection with its humanitarian work.

First Certificate Awarded _10·6·41_

Arthur Stanley.
Chairman.

No. W.S.3/ **9387**

J. C. Davies
Secretary.

A Red Cross card recording Kathleen Mitchell's service with the society. Recognition of civilian contributions in the form of cards, certificates and so on were important throughout the war.

which they filled with American soldiers. I remember my mother used to have to go round the grounds at 10 o'clock at night, shining her torch in the bushes and getting the girls back indoors.'

Families were changed by their experiences not least because of the mixing of socially and geographically defined groups of people who would never otherwise have met or known anything about each other's lives. Initial shock at each other's values, habits and even accents was in time replaced by a mutual understanding and tolerance which had an enormous impact on the prevailing values of the immediate post-war period.

'Winning the Peace', a phrase in common usage from 1941, was a popular topic of public discussion, particularly that the mistakes that followed the Armistice of 1918 should not be repeated. So expectations were high, even unrealistic, and throughout the conflict popular songs referred to an idealised peacetime. And just as all those old enough still remember the day war broke out, so they remember 8 May 1945, the day peace in Europe (VE Day) was declared. Bertha Catesby: 'The night the war was over, we found our last firelighter and called at all the neighbours' houses and lit a bonfire. A week later we had a party and we all dressed up in fancy clothes. I went as a schoolgirl in gymslip and my neighbour, a sea captain, went in my evening dress.'

From as early as 1942 the talk was of peace and what it would bring. Lux soap was more concerned with women looking as lovely as they had when their men folk had left to fight overseas.

However, peace brought new difficulties. Many married women with families had been single parents while their husbands were away in the forces. Some children born during wartime saw their de-mobbed fathers as strangers and interlopers, which inevitably put a strain on family relationships. Many couples married before and during the war found themselves each so changed by their experiences that peacetime brought them back together as strangers. As a result, after the war, divorce rates soared to double that of 1930. Two-thirds of all petitions for divorce filed in 1945 were for adultery. The armed forces in particular, at the end of the war, were able to obtain a version of the 'quickie' divorce to cope with the flood of serving men and women whose marriages were in retrospect, by mutual agreement, a mistake. But most wartime marriages and enforced separations did not end in tears or quickie divorces once peace came. People got back together and, relieved and grateful that they had survived, many had their families and lived long and happy lives together.

In 1944, Marjorie Meath's husband wrote from a transit camp to say that he was coming home.

Panic stations! I had no home for him so went to the housing department. What with having been bombed out, my husband in the army and me in the fire service, we had more than enough points for a house, even though they were in short supply.

We were allocated the house I still live in today – my husband died in 1985. Anyway, the house was in a filthy state, so Mum and I spent hours scrubbing, scraping and washing. The Blue Watch all came round on their day off and tidied the front and back gardens, without being asked, such was the spirit in our watch.

I had salvaged some furniture from our bombed flat and had stored it for four years with my sister-in-law, so I needed a day off when the removal men brought it round. I put in for a day off but the reply came, 'Permission refused'.

The men of Blue Watch said to go sick, so I did. On returning, I had to accompany a CO to an American camp and on the way, he said to me, 'Are you better, Meath?' I answered, 'Better? I haven't been ill, Sir.' I could have bitten off my tongue. But he laughed and asked if I had managed to move it all in. I was so relieved not to be on a fizzer.

I put in for discharge and was accepted so I was at home when my husband arrived back in England in July 1945. We had not seen each other for four and a half years. I sent him a little map to show where we lived.

Our daughter Janet was born in August 1946. Because her father was still in the army and I had been in the fire service, we had points towards allowances for her birth. So I had to pay just one shilling (5p) for hospital care. A baby for a shilling! Cheap at the price.

Olive Owens was another of these happy endings, although she and her husband experienced many hardships during the war:

Olive Owens on her wedding day.

MINISTRY OF AGRICULTURE AND FISHERIES

WOMEN'S LAND ARMY,

~~6, CHESHAM STREET,~~

No.: SLOANE 9822

9, Belgrave Square, ~~LONDON, S.W.1~~
London, S.W.1.

AC/MG/SL 69236

25th October, 1950.

Dear Doreen,

    I have received a letter from Her Majesty The Queen's Private Secretary asking me to convey to all who took part in the Women's Land Army Farewell Parade The Queen's congratulations and Her Majesty's gratitude for the gifts of flowers and produce.

    The Queen was very pleased with the Parade and felt it was in every way a fitting climax to the notable history of the Women's Land Army.

    May I add my personal congratulations to you and say how proud we all felt of your smart bearing and cheerful spirit.

            Yours sincerely,

Chief Administrative Officer.

The WLA was needed for another five years after the war ceased. At the end of 1950, the Land Army stood down. When Queen Elizabeth (now the Queen Mother) reviewed the WLA at a farewell parade at Buckingham Palace, Doreen Rapley (née Crane) was among the participants.

I met my husband, a Canadian soldier, during the war when I was 15. It was in a black-out outside what is now Wilkinson's in Croydon. We made a date to meet outside the Regal for the next evening, neither of us knowing what the other looked like – but I knew he was very tall.

I was to wear a blue ribbon in my blonde hair to be recognisable. He was late but then I saw this soldier peeping out from behind the recess where the exit doors were. It was him! He obviously liked what he saw – we were married four months after my 17th birthday.

We had a lovely white wedding but the day after, he had to go overseas. That was when I decided to join the civil defence as an air raid warden. I saw my husband once, a few months after our wedding. D-Day was drawing near. He was stationed on the other side of London, and so I took the train from Kingston station.

An air raid was in progress. The train stopped once; we passengers laid on the floor and were covered in glass, scratches, and bruises but the train carried on after a few minutes.

I changed trains at Clapham Junction, just in time to be blown off my feet by another bomb. I finally made it to my husband's camp, filthy, dirty and almost totally deaf, only to find our only contact was to be with a wire fence between us.

Four months after D-Day, I was with my husband for three days. After that, I did not see him again until I was shipped out to Canada to join him in March 1946, on the old ship *Aquitania*. The voyage was horrendous – storms and gales, it put me off cruises for life!

Canada was beautiful. We stayed until 1950, when we returned to Kingston, where we lived happily ever since.

In the post-war period, life was not immediately idyllic for Olive: 'We were told we couldn't have children but when we got back to England in 1950, to my surprise, I fell pregnant and we had six children in the end. We were happily married for 56 years.'

Many couples wanted to start a family. It was a logical consequence of all those years of living apart, waiting and hoping they would survive and make a life together. Even if more women had been allowed to carry on working – and a significant number of contributors to this book were very clear that they did – the post-war baby boom would undoubtedly have happened.

Official propaganda encouraged women to return to the home and although proportionately more women were employed in Britain than elsewhere in Europe, one year after the end of hostilities, more than a million women had left their jobs, willingly or otherwise.

Pat Vaughan, a member of the Women's Land Army, was still working as a full-time rat-catcher with Harrow Council when peace came. She quickly learned the problems being female would pose in peacetime: 'Whilst working with the council, I had been given an assistant, a man who had been employed as a dustman but for some reason wasn't able to continue as such. He had known nothing about the job and I had had to teach him all he knew. The council suggested to me that as I wasn't a man, they didn't think it proper I should continue to be in charge of the operation. They proposed to promote my assistant to be in charge. I would, however, be allowed to continue in the job, but only as his assistant.' Pat left, like so many women, preferring to start a family with her demobbed husband.

Betty Wilson, who was not married at that time, was clear that after five years of flying aircraft in the Air Transport Auxiliary, she could not return to her pre-war occupation. 'Could I contemplate going back to being a typist? No. January 1945, the war was obviously coming to an end, and as it was hopeless to think of going back to Civvy Street, I resigned the ATA and joined the WVS Overseas to do welfare for troops overseas. So by May 1945, I was on a troop ship in charge of 12 girls, 120 packs of playing cards, a piano, a tea service, and a triptych, all these things given for troops overseas. And for the next five years, I was in India and then Japan with the WVS.'

Eddie Gardner remembers the way peace affected factory workers at Venner's in New Malden, Surrey. 'When the war ended most of the part-time workers left – they had not wanted to be in the factory in the first place. So initially, there were no redundancies. But by 1946, many men were being laid off as women were paid less, possibly two-thirds of the wages men received. To write now that women had a difficult time during the war would be an understatement for they worked with fortitude and tolerance, accepting shortages and discrimination, and learning new trades and practices in fearful times. Every one of them deserved a medal but even more, the everlasting thanks of all the men that they surely supported.'

Margaret Stevenson continued with her job in the furniture trade. 'Towards the end, the factory went over to making Utility furniture. They didn't have a problem with keeping on women when the war was over. They didn't want to keep on everyone but they kept you on if you were good. I enjoyed the work so I stayed on and that was that, really.' She carried on working in the furniture trade until she retired at the age of sixty-five.

The Home Front, especially the contribution women made, was quickly forgotten as thoughts turned to establishing a normal life. But this does not excuse the lack of official recognition, then and now. 'The war over, we in the Timber Corps were first to be demobilised perhaps because of the heavy work we did. Most of us had been in it for three and a half years and we all felt we had made a tremendous effort to help win the war,' says Annice Gibbs. 'We felt we were the forgotten army and were very disappointed that we did not receive a gratuity or recognition of our services.'

The phrase the 'Forgotten Army' occurs again and again in people's reminiscences – referring to the WLA, munitions workers, Civil Defence employees and just about every other identifiable group of women who helped win the war. Many have recalled with bitterness their exclusion from Remembrance Day parades, although one says that she has been invited to march as a representative of the Women's Land Army to 'make up the numbers' in recent years. Of her time making Lancaster bombers, Nellie Brook comments, 'I don't regret doing it at all but the sad thing is that I never received one penny pension. A lot of people who worked during the War in awful conditions weren't looked after when it was over.'

Postscript

That the story of Britain's women has remained largely untold is due to the same circumstances that inspired so much of their involvement: when it was over, women were no longer needed to bridge the gap. It was official and, in truth, widely supported Government policy that men, as breadwinners, should have priority when it came to jobs.

Many of the women who contributed to this book said that they would have willingly carried on working in peacetime but were not given the choice. Just as the call-up had been required for the national good, so their absence from the workplace was also required for the national good. Added to that, concentrating on the home and starting a family had their own attractions. The war had been a long interruption in people's lives. For many couples, marriage had consisted of letters passing between faraway locations, snatched days of leave between long periods of separation, during which time, one or both partners faced deadly danger.

The role played by women was not commemorated in films and books of the immediate post-war era in the way the men in the armed forces were celebrated in parades, memorials and films such as *The Dambusters*, *The Longest Day* or *Above Us the Waves*. That recognition has not been forthcoming since, such as the proposed statue of commemoration in Trafalgar Square, annoys and saddens people who have corresponded with me while writing this book. As one contributor put it, 'Personally, I think we helped to win the Peace, through sheer persistence.'

Select Bibliography

Bentley Beauman, Katharine. *Green Sleeves, The Story of WVS/WRVS*, Seeley, Service and Co., 1977

Billingham, Elizabeth. *Civil Defence in War*, John Murray and the Pilot Press, 1941

Brown, Mike. *Put That Light Out*, Sutton, 1999

Calder, Angus. *A People's War, Britain 1939–1945*, Pimlico, 1992

Graves, Robert and Hodge, Alan. *The Long Weekend*, Hutchinson, 1985

Hall, Anne. *Land Girl*, Ex Libris Press, 1993

Harrisson, Tom (ed.). *War Factory A Report by Mass Observation*, Mass Observation, 1943

National Service, HMSO publication, 1939

Man Power, HMSO publication, 1944

Mills, Jon. *Doing Their Bit*, Wardens Publishing, 1996

Mulvagh, Jane. *Vogue History of Twentieth-Century Fashion*, Viking, 1988

Nixon, Barbara. *Raiders Overhead*, Scolar/Gulliver, 1980

Sackville-West, V. *The Women's Land Army*, Imperial War Museum, 1944

Hammerton, Sir John. *The Second Great War*, 8 vols, Amalgamated Press, 1939–46

I have also referred to wartime magazines and newspapers which are too numerous to mention.

Index